BREAD OR DEATH

MEMORIES OF MY CHILDHOOD
DURING AND AFTER
THE HOLOCAUST

BREAD OR DEATH

MEMORIES OF MY CHILDHOOD
DURING AND AFTER
THE HOLOCAUST

MILTON MENDEL KLEINBERG
(MENDEL DAWIDOWICZ)

FIFTH GENERATION BOOKS

Omaha, NE

Bread or Death
Memories of My Childhood Before and After the Holocaust

©2015, Milton Kleinberg. All rights reserved. No part of this book may be used or reproduced by any means, graphic, electronic or mechanical, including photocopying, recording, taping or by any information storage retrieval system without the written permission of the publisher except in the case of brief quotations embodied in critical articles and reviews.

Photos used on the cover and throughout the book are either from the personal collections of the Kleinberg family, or used with permission from the United States Holocaust Memorial Museum Archives as noted. Historical references, timeline and discussion questions were created in conjunction with the Institute for Holocaust Education in Omaha, Nebraksa.

The views or opinions expressed in this book, and the context in which the images are used, do not necessarily reflect the views or policy of, nor imply approval or endorsement by the United States Holocaust Memorial Museum.

Fifth Generation Books titles may be ordered from your favorite bookseller.
www.fifthgenbooks.com

Fifth Generation Books
c/o Concierge Marketing Inc.
13518 L. Street
Omaha, NE 68137

ISBN: 978-0-9899284-3-4
ISBN: 978-0-9899284-5-8 (Mobi)
ISBN: 978-0-9899284-6-5 (EPUB)

Library of Congress Cataloging Number: 2014943633

Printed in the USA

10 9 8 7 6 5 4 3 2

Just as Turkey served as a refuge for Spanish and Portuguese Jews, Poland became the Promised Land for the persecuted Jews of Western Europe. After the Holocaust, the United States of America and Israel became the last refuge for the Jewish people. This story is to remind my descendants not to forget our family's tragic history and our ancestors' struggle to remain Jewish under the most extraordinary circumstances.

I dedicate this book to my wife Marsha, my children Hershel and Cindy, and to Cindy's husband Michael. Also to my grandchildren and their spouses: Liza and Dani, Zev and Shachar, Yossi and Shani, Natanel and Noa, Maayan and David, and Avishai. Last, but not least, to my great-grandchildren: Noam, Idan, Ayala, Raphael, Nevo, Tuvya, and Sara, who are the next link in our story of survival. And to all future additions to this expanding family.

CONTENTS

Preface i
Foreword v

1 Everybody Out 1
2 Our Family Life between the Wars 7
3 Escape. But to Where? 23
4 Icy Boat Ride to the Soviet Side 33
5 The Long, Slow Journey across Russia 47
6 Bread or Death 55
7 Welcome to the Jewel of the Orient: Samarkand 71
8 Bullies, Battles, and Bartering 83
9 We Three Musketeers 93
10 The Knife 99
11 Danger on the Black Road 117
12 I Outlasted the War 123
13 Unexpected Reunions 133
14 Aron Kleinberg Enters Our Lives 147
15 "Let's go see the rest of the world" 153
16 Lady Liberty Beckons 169

Our American Story 181
Epilogue 199
Teacher's Guide 207
Book Club Study Questions 209
Glossary 219
Timeline 223
Acknowledgments 231
About the Institute for Holocaust Education 233
About the Author 235
Index 237
Gallery 241

PREFACE

Az m'lebt der lebt men ales.
(If you live, you live to see it all.)

Once upon a time there were many hundreds of thriving Jewish communities in Poland, and for a thousand years they contributed immensely to Poland's cultural and economic life. Now only tombstones in neglected old Jewish cemeteries from before the war remain. No individual tombstones exist for the three million Polish Jews who perished at the hands of the Nazis during World War II. Only mass graves and some isolated monuments stand.

Jews have all but been erased from the Polish consciousness. It's as though we were never there. Jews, who were a big part of Polish life, are now merely a footnote to Poland's history.

My family is one of those footnotes. And this book tells our story for the world so no one will ever forget.

My family's history in Poland dates back to the fifteenth century, but on September 1, 1939, at the start of World War

II, our long history there was about to come to an abrupt and violent end. Of the one hundred five souls that comprised our immediate family in Poland before the war, only a few survived. I among them.

Longevity has its own reward, but my seventieth birthday in 2007 marked a significant benchmark in my life, which meant that against all odds, I was alive and doing well.

The speech I wrote for my family birthday celebration started me thinking about life during the war. My grandchildren were going to Poland with their schools to visit the concentration camps and wanted to know how their grandparents and great grandparents survived the Holocaust in Poland.

This story is my attempt to answer some of their questions. Certain events my parents and I never shared with anyone except on rare occasions. Some events are too painful to talk about or make no sense telling them out of context.

I wrote this story from a child's perspective. I was, after all, just a child when the Nazis forced us into the street with just a few items on our backs and took everything we owned except our instinct for survival.

My focus is on the war years, which means my memory is stretched some seventy years. Consequently I had to do some research for dates, names, and places.

I recall vividly many of the life-and-death events I describe as though they occurred yesterday. Events I have not personally witnessed were told and retold in private conversations around the table in the German DP (displaced persons) camps. These painful recollections came to life in conversations before the scars had a chance to heal. These events—but not always the exact time or place when they happened—are deeply fixed in my mind. The scars, both mental and physical, remain.

My grandchildren, as they were growing up and wondering about our Jewish heritage and our family's experiences in Poland during World War II, asked to hear my story. And from time to time at the dinner table, I would relate bits and pieces. Here, now, is my story in full.

Background to War

Germany suffered great humiliation at the end of World War I. The Treaty of Versailles, signed June 28, 1919, made Germany accept responsibility for causing all the loss and damage of the war. As a result, it was forced to pay war reparations, surrender conquered territories, give up its air force, and greatly reduce its army. These were difficult provisions for a once proud country to accept.

Hitler was appointed Chancellor of Germany in January 1933 by President Paul von Hindenberg. Hitler, along with many others, believed that Jewry (Jews, collectively) controlled Germany's wealth and sought world domination. So when a scapegoat was needed for Germany's ills, the Jews became the focus for the Nazis.

Nazi ideology embraced two concepts. One was Lebensraum *(German living space). Because Hitler sought to expand Germany beyond regaining territory lost in WWI, German troops invaded Poland on September 1, 1939, including the author's small town of Pabianice, to gain*

Lebensraum *and to regain German territory, the Polish Corridor and Posen, given to Poland in the Treaty of Versailles.*

The other concept was the supremacy of the Aryan race. Nazi racial views saw Aryans as a superior race and Jews as inferior and destructive. Jews, of course, are not a race of people, yet Hitler was able to convince much of the world that this was true.

The German invasion of Poland officially marked the start of World War II.

FOREWORD

The Holocaust was one of the darkest times in human history. When human beings did unthinkable atrocities to each other; when an entire people were persecuted for their beliefs. A time of mass genocide; a time of countless small evils.

This gripping story of a single family captures the experiences of that generation. It is the story of love, sacrifice, and incredible courage. It is the story of an uncompromising faith that the forces of evil will not triumph.

What can we learn from a young boy?

Though just a child, Milton Kleinberg acted with determination and heroism. Despite the tragedies and cruelty, he stood up and defended himself and others. Milton's refusal to become bitter, to never give up, and to never look at himself as a victim – can inspire all of us today.

His words – "Shine a light on evil" – should be etched on all of our souls.

Evil takes many forms – it can be a sword-carrying soldier or a bullying elementary school kid. In all cases, evil will not disappear of its own accord. Perhaps the primary responsibility of educators is to teach students to stand up for what they believe is right. We cannot be passive in the face of injustice.

The Jewish People have shown through their history that darkness can never triumph. The most significant moment in our history, the Exodus from Egypt, when a slave people miraculously marched out to freedom, has become a worldwide symbol of hope for the powerless. This belief, that tomorrow does not have to look like today, that we can and must make a better world, has been our gift to the world.

Above all, *Bread or Death* teaches us that it is possible to "Shine a light on evil." We will all encounter evil in our lives. It is a lesson ever relevant for us, and never more so than today.

Rabbi Aryeh Ben David
Director of *Ayeka*: Soulful Jewish Education

1

EVERYBODY OUT

Eight days after the war started, *stomp, stomp, stomp,* the German soldiers marched in lockstep down our cobblestone streets. When we heard those jack boots resounding, my parents feared the Germans would organize a massacre (known as a *pogrom*) or come at night, round us all up into the synagogue, and set it ablaze.

I would lie in bed in our attic apartment in Pabianice, Poland, and shiver when I heard the boots marching by. When the sound trailed off into the distance, we were relieved. I was three years old, and my brother, Hershel, was two. Mother called the Germans "devils" whenever she heard the marching boots. We were scared.

The presence of the German soldiers in our small town weighed heavily on us. As the number of invasion forces on the ground increased, so did the number of restrictions and anti-Jewish laws. Consequently, our freedom to move about our town became more and more controlled.

We were hated for no other reason except that we were born Jewish. We were made to exist on the fringe of society and subjected to intimidation in the streets and little by little stripped of our dignity and human rights—and eventually uprooted from our homes.

We had often been told to get ready for resettlement. But resettlement to where? The answer was always, "You'll find out when you get there!"

Some families talked about moving in with relatives in the big city of Warsaw, some fifty miles away, or fleeing to the countryside. Others applied for visas to go to other countries.

Every family had plans how to flee should the Germans come for us, though we never thought it would come to that. Until it did.

One chilly early morning in December 1939, the devils came in trucks. The troops clambered out of the truck beds and hit the street running in those jack boots stomping on the cobblestones. The noise woke everyone up.

My father, Chaskiel, my mother, Fajga, and Hershel and I looked out the windows and saw the armed soldiers surrounding the area. Then the boots stomped up our wooden stairs. We panicked.

"*Alle raise*," (everybody out), the soldiers screamed as they pounded on our door with the butts of their rifles.

They forced themselves into our apartment and told us to pack up and go. Like our neighbors, we were ordered to take only a certain amount of possessions. They didn't give us much room to think or to do anything else. We feared they would kill us.

We had willingly signed up for relocation like the rest of the poor, so we expected that when the soldiers came, they would give us the money and take us over to the train station without force. We thought we would have time to pack. We did not realize we were going to be rushed and manhandled as if we were criminals.

It was a shock because we were expected to be given 50 zloty that had been promised us by the community. Back then 50 zloty wasn't a fortune, maybe enough for a nice meal or two.

The Germans viciously pushed us around, their bayonets constantly poking and prodding us along.

My mother was screaming. My father, on the other hand, was calm. He told her, "Quiet down, it isn't going to help anything."

We boys were, of course, crying; we didn't know what was happening. It was very scary seeing these uniformed men with guns.

We were allowed to take only the bare minimum each person could carry. Father had two bags wrapped around him and tied with a rope. Mother had wrapped some items in pillowcases. She was pregnant and struggled to carry a small suitcase and Hershel in her arms.

I was given a small cooking pot and pillow stuffed with clothes to carry.

The soldiers hauled us all out and rounded us up with our bundles and suitcases along with our neighbors and their meager possessions. We were arranged in a long line, four abreast, and all together we were marched through the center of town down to the railroad station.

Jews in Pabianice, Poland, were forced out of their homes and marched through town to the train station. Although the author and his family were forced out in 1939, this photo of a similar event in Pabianice was taken in 1942. This photo is from the United States Holocaust Memorial Museum, courtesy of Regina Frant Stawski.

Like the author's family, these Poles were forced from their homes by German police. They carry their belongings to the train station during a resettlement action. This photo is from the Instytut Pamieci Narodowej, courtesy of Jozef Marcinkowski.

In the line I saw an SS officer coming my way, so I put the cooking pot over my head. The officer lifted the pot and started laughing, and in German shouted, "*A blonde Jude*" (blonde Jew)! He then put the pot back on my head.

The Germans confiscated everything we owned that we weren't carrying, yet we ended up with 50 zloty after all. It actually was a pretty good bargain. At least we had our lives.

Jewish Life in Poland

From the eleventh through the sixteenth centuries, Poland was arguably the most tolerant country in Europe toward Jews and other minorities. Jews enjoyed legally protected religious tolerance and social autonomy. Although pogroms and blood libel accusations did occur (particularly when Jews were falsely blamed for the Black Plague), the political protection and economic opportunities afforded to Jews were relatively good.

Throughout this time period, Jews from other European communities continually flocked to Poland. In fact, Jewish immigrants from Germany brought with them the German and Hebrew languages that melded to create Yiddish. By the middle of the sixteenth century, the vast majority of the world's Jews lived in Poland.

From the seventeenth century on, however, religious conflicts (Catholic Church, reactions to the Protestant Reformation) and political struggles (partition of Poland) contributed to an environment of steadily increasing anti-Semitism.

Several massacres and expulsions of Jews took place around this time. Despite the difficulties, Jews continued to live in the areas of Poland they had occupied for centuries—now as subjects of the Russian Empire.

Throughout the eighteenth century, changing policies in the Russian Empire restricted where Jews could live, forced minors into the military, and passed various laws designed to encourage assimilation and conversion of Jews. Pogroms continued to take place sporadically into the early twentieth century and after Polish independence was reestablished in 1918, following WWI.

As Poland reestablished itself in the years following WWI, it favored a farming society and distributed large parcels of land to poor Polish peasants to accomplish this. Jews and other minorities were treated as second-class citizens and were not given land. This made life precarious and further served to concentrate Jews in the cities. By WWII in the late 1930s, fully 10 percent of the population of Poland was Jewish, with even higher percentages in the cities of Krakow (25 percent) and Warsaw (over 30 percent).

2

OUR FAMILY LIFE BETWEEN THE WARS

Between World War I and the start of World War II, my parents grew up, met each other, got married, and had children.

My mother's side, the Chapcia family, lived for centuries on a small farm in Startsive, a *shtetl* (village) located in central Poland. My grandparents Reb Gabriel and Hava Chapcia had nine children: Ber, Yente, Sheindel, Bine, Azriel, Miriam, Hendel, Wolf, and Fajga. My mother, Fajga, was the youngest of the nine children. It's not clear the exact year she was born, but our best guess is that she was born on June 10, 1918, the same year Poland declared its independence.

Her parents were *frum* (pious), and her father was the *shochet* (ritual slaughterer of animals) in town. My grandmother was known by friends and relatives as *frum* Hava. She proudly claimed to be related to the great Gerrer Rebbe (a revered religious leader). Grandma Hava was at times a rigid and bitter woman. She was hard on her children and especially severe with her daughters.

The family made a living from farming and grandfather's profession as the town's *shochet*. Under the best of circumstances it was a tough and precarious existence. From a very young age everyone worked on the farm. Farming was always backbreaking work. There were chores to be done from sunrise to dusk, except for *Shabbes* (*Shabbat*) or other holidays.

Like most in the community, the Chapcia family was always short of money. Cash was needed to purchase manufactured things they couldn't barter for or make themselves. To earn extra money, Reb Gabriel and his sons raised cattle. They sold the livestock to Polish farmers in the local market. The cattle trade wasn't only hard work, it was dangerous as well. One day, the oldest son, Ber, was taking their finest cows to market. On the road he was attacked by local Poles who robbed and killed him.

The murder of Ber had a chilling effect on the family. The authorities had a good idea who those bandits were, but they just refused to do anything about it. At an early age Mother learned that anti-Semitism was deeper than just name-calling or discrimination. It must be stated that not all Poles had deep hate for Jews. Often, it was simply a competition for scarce resources among many nationalities living in Poland.

The Jewish-owned farms in Startsive were small and crowded together around the village square. All farmers had dogs, and some of them were vicious. They were generally kept chained to the fence or a post in the ground to discourage intruders. When Mother was still a young girl, she stopped and began to tease the neighbor's dog while it was drinking some dirty water. The dog attacked her, and she was severely bitten in the face.

The farmer heard the dog bark and Mother's screams, so he quickly ran out and grabbed Mother, saving her life. Mother was long in recovery, and the trauma of this incident had a long-lasting physical and psychological impact on her. From then on, she had a fear of dogs, and it also affected her language and learning skills because she was unable to concentrate. Grandma Hava was angry with Mother and showed little compassion for her suffering. The incident sharpened Mother's survival skills and made her a compassionate mother, much more so than her own mother was.

Mother's parents were literate, at least in Yiddish. They provided for the education of their sons, but not of their daughters. On several occasions Mother attempted to sign up to go to public school, but each time she was discouraged for one reason or another. One time she came to class without a pencil, paper, or book, so she was sent home. Another time she didn't have shoes, so the teacher told her to go home, get her shoes, and come back with her mother. Grandmother discouraged her from going back, and wouldn't go with her, so Mother gave up.

Mother always regretted she never had the opportunity to learn how to read and write, so she revered educated people. Even without formal education, she became skilled in trade and savvy in the art of barter. She could keep up with the best of them and do the most complicated addition and subtraction in her head. To the end of her days, she kept good track of every dollar she had.

With nine children to feed, Grandma Hava pushed her daughters out of the house and into work at a young age. Mother's fear of dogs gave her a paranoid dislike for farm life where dogs were everywhere. When Mother was ten or eleven years old, Grandma sent her to live with her older sister Sheindel, who lived in Pabianice. While Mother lived with Sheindel, she worked for a wealthy neighbor as a nanny and housekeeper.

My Mother Meets My Father

At fifteen Mother was already a pretty woman, but she looked older than her years. Mother was five feet tall, about average for women in Poland at that time. She was blessed with large dark eyes, long curly black hair, a pretty face, and a good figure. Mother's youthful features and darker complexion gave her an exotic look. She was called a *sheyne tziganke* (a pretty Gypsy).

She was pursued by several young men in the neighborhood. One of them was a man named Chaskiel, but she didn't give him much consideration until his discharge from the army.

Chaskiel (Yechezkel) Dawidowicz was born on April 15, 1911, in a *shtetl* near Startsive. His mother died when he was still young, but his father, Moshe, married again, this time to Yente, Mother's oldest sister. Moshe had nine sons, but it's not clear if any of them were from his second marriage. Chaskiel was the third youngest of Moshe's sons from his first marriage.

Moshe worked as a laborer and could barely make ends meet. Consequently, Moshe did not have the means to provide his son Chaskiel with an education, so he, too, never learned to read or write. I don't know much about my father or his side of the family. Mother just refused to talk about that side of the family, and what she did have to say was not complimentary. All she said was that Chaskiel's two younger brothers were closely attached to him and followed him around everywhere he went. In fact Mother complained that the younger brothers would come to her house expecting to be fed. They would grab the potatoes right out of her cooking pot and eat them.

At first Mother was distrustful of Chaskiel because his father mistreated her sister, Yente. She was fearful that, after she and Chaskiel got married, he might exhibit the same traits as his father. Besides, my father had no marketable skills or profession at that time. All he had was a strong back, which qualified him for hard labor. He earned a meager living as a *fierman*, hauling various types of merchandise by horse and wagon. A *fierman* was a lower-class profession and looked upon as an uncultured ruffian.

After Chaskiel was discharged from the army, he began to pursue Mother with vigor. Mother claims that at first she didn't want to have anything to do with him, but he was relentless in his pursuit of her. He had help because Yente encouraged my mother to marry her stepson.

Apparently it wasn't love at first sight. Mother wanted to find an educated man or someone with a good profession; a wealthy man would also be good. That was not meant to be. Yente pointed out to Mother that a man with Mother's desired credentials was generally looking for a woman with the same credentials, not for a poor girl with no education or family background. A deciding factor was that after the marriage they could save money and move into an empty third-floor attic apartment in the same building where her sister, Yente, and husband, Moshe, lived.

After a short courtship, in autumn of 1935 they were married. Mother claims to have been seventeen years old, and Father was then twenty-three. As was customary, they had a small wedding attended by most of their close relatives and friends. Mother remembered that mostly her side of the family attended the wedding because many lived close by. She also recalled that from my father's side of the family, his father and stepmother and two younger brothers attended.

After the wedding the young couple moved into the building where Moshe and Yente lived. The apartment was located on Koscielna 24, right in the heart of the Jewish section of town. My father was a product of the society and environment in which he grew up. As Mother later found out, life with him was full of anxiety. Chaskiel Dawidowicz had many faults. The ones that caused Mother the most anxiety were his womanizing, his propensity for liquor, and his love of raising and racing pigeons. Although, Mother had to admit, the pigeons became a good source of protein in times of hunger.

Nazis Seize Power

Most historians believe that soon after Hitler was named Chancellor, his supporters set fire to the Reichstag (German parliament) in February 1933 so he could blame the fire on the Communists— suggesting a revolt. This act frightened the country into passing the Enabling Act in March, which granted Hitler and his government broad powers. Hitler promised to use those powers sparingly, but actually used them fully to his advantage.

By the end of March, Dachau had been established as a concentration camp for political prisoners. The three and a quarter million Jews living in Poland were alarmed when their Minister of Foreign Affairs, Josef Beck, announced Poland had room for only a half million Jews. The Nuremberg Racial Laws were established in 1935.

By 1938 the German army was set in motion, and by the end of that year, Germany had annexed Austria and the Sudetenland. Next in the path were Czechoslovakia, Bohemia, and Moravia. When none of the world powers stood up to Hitler's conquests, within weeks of signing the Nazi-Soviet Non-Aggression Pact on September 1, 1939, Hitler's troops invaded Poland. This action marked the beginning of World War II.

It Was the Worst of Times in Poland

I was born on a frosty morning on January 28, 1937, in the city of Pabianice (*Pabyanits* in Yiddish), an ancient city located in Lodz province, Central Poland—four years after Hitler became Chancellor of Germany and began his rise to power. In all of Jewish history, this was one of the worst of all times and the worst of all places to be born a Jew.

At birth and later as a child, I had Slavic features: curly blond hair, blue-green eyes, and a ruddy complexion. My relatives joked that I look like a *sheygets* (non-Jewish or gentile young boy). Some had even suggested that I may have been switched at birth in the hospital. My younger brother,

Hershel, who was born a year later in Pabianice, also had blond hair and blue eyes, indicating that blond hair at birth is an inherited family trait.

The Jewish section of Pabianice was a self-contained Yiddish-speaking community with signs in store windows lettered in Yiddish using the Hebrew alphabet. Families were crowded together on narrow cobblestone streets lined with two- and three-story apartment houses.

Everything had a Jewish feel to it: the colors, the smells, the signs, and the language. The women wore ankle-length dark dresses and scarves to cover their hair. The more Orthodox women wore wigs as further head covering. The men dressed in dark baggy pants and black hats. Smells from the bakery would waft through the streets as did the less pleasant smells of the fish market in the bazaar where vendors hung their food, spices, and other goods for all to see and buy.

Everything we needed was generally within walking distance, and what goods and services weren't close by, most we just did without. We lived near the synagogue, which meant we lived close to our friends and relatives.

Although the majority of the residents of the area were Jews, there also lived among us non-Jewish Poles, ethnic Germans, and others. All of us had our special places dictated by our faces, our speech, our dress, our manners—and our religion.

Most Pabianice Jews were part of the working poor. They were workers, small shopkeepers, and peddlers. There were also, of course, those with steady incomes—self-employed artisans or craftsmen and established merchants who were part of the middle class. Most lived in the Jewish part of town by choice, and the well-off or the rich would move to the affluent part of town or Lodz.

Yiddish (*mama lushen*) was the mother tongue for 80 percent of the Pabianice Jews. Although most Jews could speak Polish and other languages, fewer than half spoke Polish fluently. Consequently, it was easy to recognize Jews in the general population. Except for the modern Jews who were integrated in the Polish society, the rest of the Jews stood out by their speech, dress, look, and manners.

My childhood memory of Pabianice before the war is scant. Warszawska was a main street where the street car ran. We lived in the apartment on Koscielna Street, which was one street over and ran parallel to Warszawska, and adjacent to a street car station. People would run back and forth to buy tickets that would take them to other parts of town or to Lodz.

From our third-floor apartment, we could hear the street car noises. The clanking and rolling of cars would get louder as the street car made its turn close to Koscielna Street. Before it stopped, we could hear the squeaky brakes and, at times, even see the sparks from the overhead electric wires.

On cold days, Hershel and I would sit with our noses glued against the kitchen window and watch the people below as they were going about their day. On Friday afternoon the hustle-bustle of Koscielna Street would slowly quiet down as the Jewish shops and businesses closed to get ready for *Shabbat*.

On Saturdays the cobblestone street was shiny, quiet, and seemed to be resting until sunset. We had plenty of friends or cousins our age to play with. Most people in the neighborhood knew us or were related to us. It was a familiar and comfortable place to live. Yet as the storm was gathering in Europe, the adults (and we children who overheard the whispered fears) hoped the madness in the world would go away.

My father was a difficult and complex man. He was quick to anger, but he was also resourceful in times of trouble, and above all he was a survivor. It was difficult to be around him, especially when he was drunk, which made him unpredictable. Sometimes he would bring his drunken Pole friends home with him, but my mother would have none of it. When hearing boisterous language or swearing in Polish on the steps, she would grab her frying pan, start swinging, and not let the drunken Poles in the house. More than once that pan of hers would graze my father or his drunken friends.

One time my mother heard my father laugh and the giggling of a young girl beneath the upstairs window. She looked out and saw him pin down a young Polish girl against the wall as she attempted to break free from his grasp. So Mother grabbed her frying pan and ran down the three flights of stairs. Before my father could turn around, she hit him on the head with her iron frying pan and knocked him out. The young girl screamed, covered her head to avoid getting hit, and ran away. My mother left him on the sidewalk. She ran up to the apartment, grabbed Hershel and me, and sought refuge with her sister Hendel, who lived a street car stop away.

When my father came to his senses, his father told him, "If you hit Fajga or my grandchildren, you will have to deal with me." But it was more with a wink of an eye than a threat in earnest. As Mother liked to say that apple didn't fall far from the tree. My mother was not a shrinking violet either; she would fight back.

On another occasion, my father came home drunk, and she questioned where he had been. He hit her saying, "It's none of your business!" Without hesitation, Mother grabbed a glass and threw it at him, hitting him in the right eye. Then she screamed at him, with the pan in her hand, "You don't hit me in front of the children!" He almost lost that eye, and for several months his eye was bandaged.

Of all of my father's vices—and there were many—the smelly pigeons he kept in the attic were the most annoying. They occupied a good part of his time and absorbed a good share of our meager resources. To him the pigeons came first; they were always given food even if there was no bread for our table.

Those "smelly pigeons," as Mother called them, were a source of contention between them. Mother was a frugal woman, and pigeons were a luxury we couldn't afford. Father's indulgences were the source of many arguments. Although, when food was in short supply, those pigeons ended up on our dinner table.

As a *fierman*, my father worked with his horse and wagon. Sometimes on short trips he would take Hershel and me with him on deliveries. That was a high point. He would buy us ice cream and tell us how to fight back when the Poles attempted to harass us. He was very specific in his instructions on when to run and when to hold your ground. Oddly enough, these instructions came in very handy in later years.

Mother would, of course, give him strict orders not to take us with him into the bar. But he would always cheat and stop in for at least one quick drink. Each time we were told not to tell Mother or his belt would come off. He was a familiar figure in the Pabianice bars, especially where other fiermen hung out.

From the earliest days, Father remained a shadowy figure in my life, hidden deep in the recesses of my childhood memories. It is strange though. To this very day, I remember the smell of his breath and the sting of the belt when it came off his waist, but not what he looked like.

Nazi-Soviet Non-Aggression Pact

Both Germany and Soviet Russia had lost power and territory at the conclusion of WWI. As Hitler considered his plans to invade Poland in order to restore and gain territory, he saw an opportunity to ensure that the Soviets would not object and force him to fight a multi-front war.

So on August 23, 1939, Nazi Foreign Minister (von Ribbentrop) and the Soviet Foreign Minister (Molotov) signed the Nazi-Soviet Non-Aggression Pact, also known as the Ribbentrop-Molotov Pact. The agreement had an initial term of ten years (subject to extension) and stated that the Soviet Union would remain neutral in a European War, and that Germany would not get involved in the battles taking place between the Soviet Union and Japan.

The pact also had a secret protocol that divided Eastern Europe into German and Soviet "spheres of influence."

In addition, the agreement divided Poland (as well as Romania, Lithuania, Latvia, Estonia, and Finland) into Nazi and Soviet "spheres of influence." As soon as news of the pact was released, people in these countries knew that invasion would come quickly.

We all knew our world was about to change—even for me as a child—but no one foresaw what was to come. No one imagined the Germans, generally regarded as a cultured nation, were actually preparing for the massacre of the entire Jewish people.

Panic reigned in the streets. The Polish Army had started to requisition everything that moved: buses, taxis, the few private cars, trucks, *droshkies* (open carriages), horses, and wagons. My father had his horse and wagon requisitioned, but was told to hold on to them until needed.

We went to the train station to say goodbye to my Aunt Hendel's oldest son, who was in his uniform and was required to go back to his military unit of the Polish Army in Warsaw. There we saw husbands and wives, parents and sons saying goodbye and crying. Everywhere quick-thinking women formed long lines in front of grocery stores. They began to stock up on food knowing that the war would bring shortages—and much horror we could never have anticipated.

At the start of the German occupation, getting out was still possible, but where would we go? Some went to larger cities like Lodz or Warsaw, others to the countryside, and many made their way to the Russian border. Those who stayed behind and those who had returned from the Soviet side saw the Jewish neighborhood being completely enclosed. Jewish businesses were confiscated and handed over to ethnic Germans.

We kept hearing positive reports about the German invasion on Polish radio. Unfortunately, none of them were true. Yet we still didn't believe the Germans would treat Jews that badly. They certainly had treated the Jews better than the Russians did during World War I.

When the Germans occupied Pabianice on Rosh Hashanah, they destroyed our synagogue and turned it into a stable. Then they started to isolate the Jews from the rest of the population. In October a Judenrat (Jewish leadership and liaison to the occupying Germans) had been formed. Immediately the Jews were ordered to select people for resettlement. Each family that voluntarily signed up were promised 50 zloty. The poor were the first to sign up. Among them were my father and his father, Mother's sisters, and several other relatives. We did not get the money until we were forced to resettle in January 1940.

Poland Divided

Once the Nazi-Soviet Non-Aggression Pact was signed, it took the German forces a mere week to invade Poland (September 1, 1939). This attack had been planned well in advance, and the German troops mounted a massive attack from the north, west, and south. Tanks and aircraft were used extensively. The Polish Army had only begun to prepare for war and was not equipped to handle the aggressive German tactics (also known as "blitzkrieg" or "lightning war").

Within two days of the invasion, Britain and France declared war on Germany. Interestingly, they did not declare war on the Soviet Union despite its alliance with Nazi Germany.

Two weeks later (September 17, 1939) the Soviets (Russian Red Army) invaded Poland from the east. The Polish Army was completely out-numbered and out-equipped. By September 27, 1939, the Polish Army in Warsaw surrendered to the Germans, and the Polish campaign was over. Less than a week later, the German and Soviet forces gained complete control of Poland, dividing it between them at the river Bug.

The river Bug (pronounced boog) became the dividing line, the border between the German-occupied portion of Poland and the Soviet zone of occupation.

3

ESCAPE. BUT TO WHERE?

ate would bring me face to face with death many times over the course of my family's survival odyssey. Death had now become an everyday thing. It was an unwanted but inescapable companion.

The first time I saw a Jew being murdered was when we were on the train taking us from our hometown to the border. An old woman right next to us just sat down on the platform and cried rather than follow orders to board the train. She did not want to go.

A Nazi officer took out his holstered pistol and shot her point blank in the head. Her brain splattered all over us.

The German soldiers herded us onto smelly boxcars, which were recently used to transport cattle. It appeared that the cattle were just unloaded and we were taking their place. After our thirty-six-hour journey without food, water, or sanitation, the cattle cars stopped and dropped us off in Siedlce, an old Jewish town located about 90 kilometers (55 miles) east of Warsaw.

Men and women carry their bundles of possessions and board resettlement trains in an unidentified Polish city. This photo is from the United States Holocaust Memorial Museum, courtesy of Heide Brandes.

One of the SS guards asked if anyone understood German, and many nodded their heads yes. He then said Herr Hitler had designated the other side of the river as the new Jewish homeland. Someone asked if the Russians knew this.

"Of course," he said. "The negotiations are still going on."

No one really believed him. He also said in earnest, "You should all go across the river Bug at Terespol to the Bolsheviks' side; it's about 20 kilometers north of here. Do it soon before the Bolsheviks close the border!"

Map of Poland in 1931 showing Pabianice, Lodz, Warsaw, Brest, and the river Bug.

That was true. Many of us wanted to get across the river, but deciding how to get there was the real challenge, especially during winter. The city of Brest was an important border crossing point because it is situated on the main railway line connecting Berlin and Moscow. All railway transportation going east beyond Brest (leaving Poland and entering Russia) must have their cars changed because the Russian rails are a broader gauge than the European tracks. This meant the Brest Bridge crossing area on both sides of the river was heavily guarded. The Russians, however, kept their side open for a short period for those fleeing the German side.

From the train drop-off point, the Nazis marched us, with our luggage in hand, about 10 kilometers (6 miles) in the direction of an old Jewish town whose synagogue had recently been burned by the Germans with the help of some townspeople.

When we saw the burned synagogue, an incredible fear came over us. The stench of death lingered in the burned remains of the devastated *shul* (synagogue).

A synagogue burned by the Nazis similar to the one where the author and his family sought refuge. Photos from Yad Vashem archive.

We were among at least a couple hundred people that the Germans marched there. No one wanted to go in to what was left of the synagogue. The cinders were still smoldering. We were all hungry, thirsty, and tired. The Nazi soldiers told us there was water and food inside, but it might not be there long, so we went in. We were fearful that once we are all in the building, the Germans would set the synagogue on fire again.

The shell of the synagogue was not big enough to hold everyone inside, so some people ended up outside, exposed to the elements in the adjacent cemetery.

My mother's sisters and their families, who were deported with us, were already inside. Mother was bewildered. She had Hershel in her arms, and I was hanging on to her skirt. All of us were being herded like cattle into the smoldering synagogue by Nazi soldiers at rifle point.

My father seemed to have been unshaken by this whole experience. With his two bags over his shoulders, tied by rope, he took Hershel from Mother and grabbed my hand. Then with a sober face and gentle voice said; "*Shah* (quiet), children. Everything will be better tomorrow."

We found a place in a corner on the second floor next to mother's sisters and their families. The roof of the *shul* was burned out so we might as well have been outside ourselves, but my parents did manage to find a little place where the roof came to an angle that offered some shelter from the weather for our family.

Father put down the packs from his shoulders and went to find some food and water. When he came back, he told Mother, "Fajga, take the food and share it with the children. Tomorrow I will find us some more food, and we will start looking for a way to get us across the river to the Soviet side."

His behavior during that period was so out of character that it has stuck with me to this very day. Those were the kindest and most reassuring words I remember him ever saying to us children. He was like a rock of stability during that awful time.

That cold January 1940 we all had to decide what to do next. Do we all go back to Pabianice, or go across to the Russian side? My father made it clear that we were going across the river even if we all had to swim.

My father's father and stepmother were more fearful of the godless Communists than of the Germans and pointed out that during World War I the Germans were more humane to Jews than the Russians had been.

My father said, "At least the Communists accept Jews, but the Nazis say that they plan to kill all the Jews."

Moshe said, "That's nonsense! How are they going to kill millions of Jews? I had heard the Rabbi say, 'Hitler says such things for political purposes and will back off once the war in Poland is over.'"

My father replied to him, "You listen to those religious mavens (experts) too much. Those Rabbis spend all day in the synagogue studying yesterday, but know nothing of today's world. Whenever self-defense conversations took place in the past, the Rabbis were the first to be against it. All I know is what I see, the Germans were given orders to kill Jews, and they are doing it. I would gladly pay attention to the Rabbis if they said we need to organize and defend ourselves."

During our brief stay in that burned synagogue, there were many such heated discussions on whether to go back or whether to cross the river Bug. In the end Mother's three sisters, Hendel, Yente, and Sheindel, and their families joined a group of like-minded Jews who went back to Pabianice. After they left, we never saw or heard from them again.

We later were told that within a month our Jewish neighborhood had been turned into a closed ghetto that housed about eight thousand men, women, and children. All our relatives who remained behind in Pabianice perished. As it turned out, compared to what our relatives had to endure, we were among the lucky ones who got out in time.

The Angel of Death Comes

A strange event that haunts me to this very day occurred during our short stay in that burned-out *shul* (synagogue).

A white-bearded man wrapped in a *talit* (prayer shawl) stood next to the scorched *bema* (platform on which religious services were conducted) and looked as though he was deeply engrossed in a loud conversation with an invisible person. People in the *shul* ignored him and attributed his behavior to grief. Apparently his wife and son had been in the *shul* and burned alive when the Germans torched the building.

Afterward this old-looking man felt the angel of death was after him, so he was attempting to convince the angel of death that he was not ready to give in.

Hershel and I approached the man and asked to whom he was talking. He said in a low voice, "The angel of death!"

We were mystified. "But where is he? We can't see him."

He answered, "Only I can see him!"

He went on to tell us that the angel of death comes down from above and takes the souls of people who are about to die with him. He told us, "If you recite the *Shemah* (a Jewish prayer) when he comes for you, he can't take you. I don't want to go with him, so he attempts to trick me into stop praying. The angel can't touch me as long as I pray and don't fall asleep."

He introduced himself, but I don't recall his name. However, in my dreams he calls himself Abraham. During the conversation he would stop several times and recite the *Shemah* again. I told him my name was Mendel and my brother's name was Hershel. He then told us that he, too, had a son named Mendel who was twelve years old, but the boy and his mother had died in the *shul* fire.

"Both of them died here next to the *bema*! Now the angel of death wants to take me, but I won't let him." He then said, "I will give each of you boys a zloty every time you wake me when you see me falling asleep. If one of you can stay up and talk to me when I begin to doze off, that will keep me awake."

When we told our parents about our conversation with Abraham, Mother was upset. Chaskiel was more upbeat. He said, "Fajga, let the boys earn a couple zloty. Besides how long can this old man last?"

Well, Abraham lasted for two more days, and all that time he ran around the *shul* arguing with the angel of death.

Hershel and I each woke him up twice. In the evening of the second day he took off his *talit*, folded it in a nice even square, put his prayer book down on top of his *talit*, and said to us that the angel of death would soon take him.

Abraham looked at us with eyes of anguish and said, "The angel of death has showed me the future, and I want no part in it!"

He brought his few belongings over and gave them to Mother. "I will no longer need them, and do with them as you please." To Father he gave the zloty he had wrapped in a white handkerchief and told him to use the money to buy passage to cross the river to the Russian side.

Abraham looked at us as though he were a prophet of years gone by, and in a resolute voice repeated, "Cross the Bug to Russia! Here there is nothing but death waiting for all of you. On the other side there is hope and life."

At sundown, this lonely old Jew said his prayers for the last time. Abraham lay down on the charred floor next to the *bema* with his jacket rolled up to make a pillow. He placed his prayer book carefully on top of his jacket and then he rested his head on the prayer book and died.

My father found a Rabbi who knew Abraham and said *Kaddish* (mourner's prayer) for him. With Abraham's death, it seemed as if ten centuries of Jewish history in Poland died with him because Jews had lived in Poland and had been part of the fabric of the country. Now my family and Abraham, I was to realize later, were the last generation to call Poland our home. We all agreed that Abraham would be pleased that we were present when the Rabbi recited the *Kaddish* eulogy at his funeral.

Abraham's imagined fight with the angel of death must have sparked a premonition in my mother that she then shared with me. It was a defining moment for me and for my mother because she knew that we would never see our relatives again. She just had that feeling. The angel of death had been so close to us that we knew something was going to happen. And both Hershel and I felt that somehow we were going to be guided by Abraham.

Lesser of Two Evils

Both the Nazis and the Soviets sought to destroy Polish culture and national identity.

The Nazis believed the first step to destroying the Polish people would be to destroy the Jews. Jews and other Polish minorities were massacred. Millions more were sent to ghettos, forced labor camps, and concentration camps.

The Soviets' main tool in this endeavor was "Sovietization"—the use of propaganda to forcibly instill a Soviet culture and mentality. When Sovietization techniques did not seem sufficient, resettlement to forced labor camps in eastern Russia was used. It is important to note that the Soviets used similar tactics with all Poles who seemed to pose a threat, or who opposed becoming Soviet citizens. This meant that Jews were not generally targeted for harsher treatment, and in fact, anti-Semitism was technically unlawful.

According to Marxist thinking the collective ownership of land and resources eliminated the struggle between the worker and the industrialists—everyone was considered equal. Collective farms and redistribution of property were carried out by the occupying Soviet forces.

The NKVD (People's Commissariat for Internal Affairs) was the law enforcement of the Soviet Union, handling everything from traffic police to protecting the borders. They carried out mass executions, mass deportations, and political assassinations particularly of people who were enemies of Stalin. One of their most noted victims was Leon Trotsky, a Russian Marxist revolutionary.

In 1940–1941 the NKVD carried out four mass deportations of nearly one and a half million Poles to Siberia and other inner remote areas of the Soviet Union. Poles were considered enemies of the Soviet Union and a threat to its existence. The NKVD is often compared to the KGB (Committee for State Security) of 1954–1991.

4

ICY BOAT RIDE TO THE SOVIET SIDE

The weather was cold that winter, but the ice on the river Bug was too thin to walk across and difficult for maneuvering a boat. Yet my father befriended a Polish border guard who was also a pigeon lover. He bribed the guard with some cash and a bottle of vodka for him to take us across the river in his boat.

One mild, opportune evening, the guard told us to load the boat, gave us two more oars, and told Father and Mother they must help him row our family across the river.

We crossed the river on a rickety old, flat-bottomed wooden boat with green paint chipping off the sides. The boat was definitely not meant for five people but we all managed to squeeze into it. There was a bench in the back and a bench in the front for sitting. Mother and Father manned one set of oars; the guard took the other set.

The escort told us, "Don't move, don't shake the boat in any way, and don't cry or make any noise." He also said, "I'm not as much worried about the Soviets as the Germans. The Germans will shoot without asking questions."

It was a precarious crossing. Ice was all around us. As if the crossing was not scary enough, Father was sort of kidding me, saying, "Remember if something happens you're going to have to swim," knowing full well I didn't know how to swim. I was scared to death.

Then he made it worse by saying, "When you swim, remember your brother doesn't know how to swim, so you're going to have to keep an eye on him." Just the thought of being in the cold water terrified me.

Wary as I was already with those worries, there were several other things of concern, too. One was that the boat was leaking, not a lot but enough that my feet were getting cold and wet. My mother rubbed my feet to try to get them warm and dry. At one point my father grabbed a long sock from his bag and started plugging up certain parts of the boat that had sprung leaks. He had something like a spoon to push the sock into one of the holes.

To make matters worse, the current pushed us too far down river. We needed to land where the escort had arranged things with a border guard, but we were off course and landed at a different spot than planned.

When we finally reached the shore, I grabbed the sock, and the boat almost instantly filled with water.

On the other side was the city of Brest, but the guard had dropped us off about 10 kilometers (6 miles) south of the bridge crossing, and there we ran into a Russian guard. Our escort told Father to give the Russian a bottle of vodka. Father hesitated, but Mother grabbed the bottle from his pack and gave it to the Russian. When the Russian hesitated, Mother grabbed my father's last bottle of vodka and handed it over too. Then the Russian stretched out his hand and helped us out of the boat.

He told us the border was now closed and gave us directions to the synagogue located in the Jewish section of town. Polish Jews and non-Jews in great numbers were crossing the Bug to the Soviet side in order to escape the Nazis. The Germans wanted the Soviets to enforce the Soviet-German pact and close the border. We were among the last to cross at that spot.

We walked about six miles to the Jewish section of town where we hoped to blend in with others attempting to leave Poland. The synagogue provided us with some bread and cheese and a place to stay. No one could escape the watchful eye of the NKVD. They were everywhere wearing armbands and sidearms with suits and coats, not military uniforms.

Within days, we were arrested and transported by truck north to a holding camp or prison near Bialystok. We were now among a large number of Poles and Jews who were considered reactionaries, whatever that meant. The NKVD made us register where we were from. As such, we were categorized as prisoners of the Soviet Union, which meant we would be deported to a labor camp in Siberia.

The authorities tried convincing us to become citizens of the Soviet Union. They claimed we would get more bread, would be issued passports, and that life would be easier.

My parents were of two different minds about whether they should accept Russian citizenship. My mother said, "No, if I become a citizen, they won't let me go back."

My father said, "What's the difference?"

She argued absolutely not, because she planned to go back to Poland. She had a certain intuitive sense. She could neither read nor write, but she had that innate sense about what she had to do. The interesting thing about her is that she did not think much about consequences, she knew what she must do and she did it.

Hundreds of us were sandwiched in an old, cement floor warehouse in Bialystok. The building was elevated to protect it from flooding by a river that ran nearby. There were windows in the structure but very few. The only place to store our possessions was on the floor. There were no bunks, so we slept on the floor next to our things.

In spite of the harshness of the conditions in the holding camp, we had to admit that the Russians treated us much more humanely than did the Germans. At registration, each member of the family was issued new Russian identification papers and food ration cards. These ration cards were good everywhere.

We were subject to immediate deportation within two hours' notice. So we had our bags packed and were ready for departure when called. Departures took place twice a week, sometimes more often. We were in the Bialystok holding camp for about a month when our names were called.

Deportation on Boxcars

In February 1940 we were ordered to board the trucks that took us to the train station. As we were getting off the trucks, we could see a long train with dark smoke coming from the locomotive. The engine had about fifteen to twenty boxcars attached behind.

At the transit point we were processed and assigned to a specific boxcar with other Jewish and Christian families. From there we were marched with our meager possessions to the loading station. For many of us this was the second forced train trip, and no one knew what to expect. Most of the passengers being deported by the Russians were Polish citizens.

At first, the reasons given by the Russians for deporting us varied and ranged from being capitalist, or counterrevolutionary, to harboring some other imagined anti-Soviet political agenda. In reality, we were only bewildered, poor Polish farm peasants and Jews who had lost everything fleeing from the Nazis' atrocities.

Refugees board a deportation train for labor camps in Siberia. This photo is from the National Archives and Records Administration, College Park.

The Russian boxcars were larger than the Polish cars and free of the cattle stink. The car was divided in half, leaving a walkway between two rows of makeshift wooden bunks. Most importantly, they had some minor amenities including a potbelly stove in the middle of the boxcar. There were water buckets, brooms, a coal shovel, and urine pans. The toilet was a v-slot on the floor next to the door. Fortunately, someone had put up a flimsy curtain to give some semblance of privacy for the thirty to forty people in each car.

Apparently this train had transported Polish passengers before. The previous occupants had left their names scratched on the wooden planks of the bunk beds. We, too, carved in its planks everyone's names or initials, some in Yiddish, some in Russian, some in Polish, and some in other languages too. I was so young I could not even write my full name yet. But I knew how to make the "M," and that is what I carved.

The boxcar had two small square windows up high in each corner of the car. To see out, we had to sit on the top bunk. Those small windows provided most of the light during daytime.

People moved slowly, no shoving, no conversations. With gloomy faces, and their bundles under their arms, they quietly selected their bunks. Children hung onto their parents and, bewildered, shuffled along into the car. A Russian guard checked off names on his list. About thirty-five people, including children, were assigned to our car. An NKVD officer and his assistant walked to the middle of the car.

The officer started to speak in a stern voice, then he took a good look at the dejected group before him, and his tone of voice changed. In a normal voice he said, "You are all prisoners of the USSR. If you do what is asked of you and keep your noses clean, you will be treated well."

The officer and his assistant guard jumped off the train, and before closing the large sliding door he shouted, "This door stays shut until one of the guards opens it." The door was locked on the outside and could be opened from the inside only in case of emergency, but no one would dare to open it unless the train went off the track or there was a fire.

There were fewer Russian soldiers guarding this train than there had been Nazis guarding us on the train in Poland. Once we were deep in Russia and at specified heavily guarded station stops, people were permitted to get off the train and scrounge for food. Of course, if you were to escape, where would you go?

Father and Mother would take turns leaving the train. At larger cities or when the locomotive was disconnected from the boxcars, it was generally safe to get off. People would exchange valuables they brought with them for food and other necessities from the locals. Father would usually come back with bread, and Mother with milk for Hershel and me.

The train's destination was to somewhere in the northern part of East European Russia. Our first stop in a major town was Leningrad (St. Petersburg), and after a short stay there, we were back on the train. This time, however, we were informed we were going to Northwestern Russian Federation, a place called Arkhangelsk. No one had heard of the place or knew exactly where it was.

In January 1940 we had been marched out of our hometown of Pabianice, Poland, fled across the river Bug into Soviet-occupied territory at Brest, Belarus. We were captured and ordered onto a cattle-car train in Bialystok, headed for a refugee camp in Arkhangelsk, Russia.

One man in our boxcar said we were going to a very cold place he described as the Siberian tundra, not far from Finland.

Forced Labor in Russia

The first of the four mass deportations of Poles and Jews by the Russians took place on February 10, 1940. Some 250,000 people boarded over a hundred trains to begin a long journey to remote areas of northwestern Russia.

The region was flat and covered by a forest of pine trees extending in all directions from town. The climate was harsh. The summers were cool; the winters very long and cold. Food and warm clothing were inadequate. From mid-May, lasting for about eighty days, was the season of white nights, and during that period, it didn't get dark.

In the midst of this remote region sat Arkhangelsk, a timber town, consisting of small wooden homes and wooden sidewalks. The deportees were put to work in a variety of ways: working in forestry or gold mines or lumber yards. Work was hard and continued for long hours. Those who could not work did not receive food. The Soviets did not worry about escape. Their prisoners were in the middle of nowhere with no place to go. Children were put into schools and taught Soviet propaganda.

We lived together as a family in a small wooden house on a *kolhoz* (collective farm). My new baby brother, Velvel, was born in Arkhangelsk in May or June 1940, and he was a healthy boy. Our home was located about six kilometers from town. My father took care of the horses housed in a barn located about 100 yards from our home. He also worked in the lumberyard in town.

Mother was in charge of planting potatoes and performing other farm duties. A gravel road in front of our house went past the barn and merged with the main road. To the right was Arkhangelsk, to the left were several small villages, and straight ahead were more collective farms and a stream.

On both sides of the gravel road from our house were large clearings of pasturelands used for grazing cattle during the summer months. When the cows grazed in the pasture near the house, Mother would run out, milk the cows, and bring the milk home for her babies.

Father warned her that if they caught her, the commissar would throw her in jail. She would reply, "What are they going to do? Send me to Siberia?" However, she did make some adjustment to her thievery by involving co-conspirators in order to gain some perceived protection. She befriended the commissar's wife and a couple of other wives and shared the looted milk with them.

Our Most Prized Possession

By this time my parents had depleted some of our possessions through trading and acquired some new things for future trades. They had traded silver, gold rings, watches and linens for food or in exchange for rubles, plates, and china.

My brother and I were young children, so from the start of our travels we had very few possessions of our own. Our most prized possession at that time was a whistle our father had made me. It was nicely carved out of wood.

When I blew the whistle, it gave off a strange sound. It sounded more like a musical instrument than a loud whistle. I would play with it often. Hershel and I would play hide and seek and whoever hid, the seeker had the whistle.

Hershel and I, just young boys about four and five years old, were enrolled in a day care kindergarten while our parents were at work. Velvel was a baby and stayed with Mother while she did farm work. At that kindergarten I took on the responsibility of an older brother. Hershel was younger, smaller, and more frail than I was. The other kids sensed it, so they would pick on him or grab his food. I would jump in, and a fight would ensue.

That year I had at least one fight a day with someone. I didn't care if they were bigger or stronger. When they picked on Hershel, they picked on me. Father had taught me how to act in a fight.

He said, "You can't act scared. The person who throws the first punch is usually the winner. If the boy is bigger, first kick him in the shins, and if he is your size, then hit him in the nose."

Mother was angry. She told me not to listen to him. But I did listen, and it did save me from getting beaten up many times. I also realized that once bullies know that you are willing to fight, they tend to leave you alone.

When we were in the children's center in Arkhangelsk, I gave Hershel the whistle to use as a signal for me to come to his rescue whenever other children hassled him, which happened quite frequently. It was not all his fault. He was just a year younger than I but much more immature and didn't realize the consequences of fighting. If he had a piece of bread, I had to wait until he finished eating it; otherwise, some kid would come and grab it.

Hershel just did all he could to survive. On his own he would not have lasted long. He needed a mother and a brother. I think his weakness or vulnerability and his dependence on me is what made me so strong because I had the responsibility of taking care of him and that is why I was able to sort of shake free of fear and confront his tormenters.

During this odyssey of being torn away from everything that I knew, and facing threats left and right, I learned to develop an attitude that served me well and that literally helped me to survive. You see, I felt I was fearless. When faced with a threat I learned that whenever possible you should take the first action before someone else does. Whenever I ran into trouble with other kids and they wanted to hurt me, I took the initiative. I hit them before they could hit me.

But I could not always hit everyone who posed a threat. Sometimes the only defense was to talk my way out of it, and if that failed, I just had to look for an exit strategy. Inside of me I carried the thought of my mother and her fierce love. Mother was relentless in making sure we understood that our survival depended on the family staying together and that we all lived for one another. That was a very important message.

She said, "As long as I've got a nail on my finger, as long as I have a voice, as long as I have legs, I will fight to make sure you and your brothers are alive." How true that turned out to be.

That small wooden whistle with a warbling marble inside remained with us up to one of our future stops. Then it was lost. More than a toy or a distress signal, the whistle connected me to my brother. It was sorely missed when we lost it. Of course, I could not know it yet, but there would come into my possession another object that would play a vital role in helping me escape two life-and-death struggles.

Warmer weather would unfortunately unleash large swarms of flies, mosquitoes, and a great variety of other vermin making life miserable. Yet long summer days with little darkness were nourishing days with plenty of food available in the wild. In the forest were abundant mushrooms, blueberries, nuts, and other edible plants; however, people who went to gather food in the woods had to be careful of wolves and not get lost. Mother would always pick blueberries and mushrooms during the season, and once she got lost.

Father and some neighbors organized a search party and looked for her for over two days. A native Russian told Father because of the long day hours and the lumber trails in the woods, many lost people end up in one of the logging camps, which were located about 20 kilometers north of town. Sure enough, when Father arrived in a lumber camp, there Mother was with a blanket around her shoulders sipping mushroom soup from a tin cup.

Long, dark winter nights brought other challenges. Mother suffered from night blindness. She had to make sure it was still daylight when she picked Hershel and me up from kindergarten. On the way home, it was usually dark, and she had to depend on us to get her home.

We lived in this strange land for over a year, and we were beginning to get used to the place. Granted, it was a difficult and cold place, but at least the bombs weren't falling, food was plentiful, and no one was shooting at us. Not yet.

The War Expands

Fighting was taking place along a thousand-mile front running roughly from Leningrad in the north to Rostov in the south of the Soviet Union. The Germans were coming closer to the larger cities of Moscow and Leningrad in 1941, and that's when the Soviet Premier Stalin ordered hundreds of factories in the Ukraine and western Russia to be evacuated east. The Kharkiv factory was moved to Nizhny Tagil by rail, and together with the Dzerzhinsky works they formed the Stalin Ural factory. This factory became the largest producer of tanks.

To run the factories, Jews and Poles alike were arrested and put into the Russian Army. They were even given uniforms, but they were not trusted. The Russians treated them like prisoners, which they were.

In December 1941 the Japanese attacked the United States by bombing Pearl Harbor in Hawaii thus drawing the United States into World War II.

Map showing fighting front and cities of Moscow, Leningrad and Archangelsk.

5

THE LONG, SLOW JOURNEY ACROSS RUSSIA

Just as we were getting familiar with our surroundings in Arkhangelsk, the war had caught up with us again. On a bright summer day in 1941 we were ordered to report to the train station with our bags packed.

The most direct route from Arkhangelsk to East Siberia and Central Asia where the labor camps were being relocated was by way of Moscow. Leningrad is located northwest of Moscow, the opposite direction from where these work camps were situated.

That summer, word passed that Leningrad was about to fall into German hands, and the *Luftwaffe* (German air force) was engaged in a heavy bombing campaign on the city. Our hopes were that somehow our train would bypass Moscow and leave the war behind. It wasn't a good time to leave, nor was it a good time to stay, but it didn't matter. The war was coming our way, and we had no say in the matter.

At the train station we were registered, issued new ration cards, and assigned to train number one. After registration we were ordered to line up four abreast and follow the official to a cargo-loading platform a short distance from the main railway station. Our train was parked next to a raised cargo platform used to load heavy cargo. The platform was at the same level as the boxcar's deck. There were several steps that led to the concrete deck, but none from the deck to the boxcar. The locomotive had at least fifteen boxcars attached.

On the platform, the soldier counted off about thirty-five names from his clipboard and told them to get on board into the empty boxcar. The rest of the people followed the soldier until all boxcars of the train were loaded. Men, women, children, and, in some cases, whole families, including grandparents, were deported together. Whenever possible, the Russians did make an effort to keep families together. Poles, both Jews and non-Jews, made up the passenger list of this train and several trains behind us. Many of the same people who had been deported to Arkhangelsk the previous year were now on the trains heading for resettlement.

Our journey to Arkhangelsk had made us more savvy travelers and gave us a good idea of what we could expect this time. Once the deportation order was announced, every family had started to make preparations for a long trip. We knew these trains were earmarked for resettlement, but no one knew their destination or how long it would take to get there.

Three possible destinations were being talked about: Siberia, the Urals, and Central Asia. Of the three, Central Asia was the preferred destination. It was mainly because Central Asia and countries with names of Uzbekistan and Tadzhikistan had warmer climates and were farthest from the fighting.

Our bundles were packed with the most practical things we could carry. In addition to the basics, such as bread, hard cheese, salami, and clothing, we carried things of value that could be converted to rubles or used as barter. Items made from silver, gold rings, and wristwatches were especially highly valued and could be traded for food. The other passengers did the same. Everyone was focused on our circumstances, the war, and how to keep our families together.

The day before we were to report for departure, Mother had managed to bribe a Russian official with some milk in order to find out what our destination would be. According to the official, train one's destination, on which we were listed, was headed to Central Asia, but the name of the city or province was left blank. He also warned Mother not to be too optimistic about the destination because those orders were subject to change at any time along the way.

Father was sure our destination was Central Asia, which turned out to be true. He thought all provinces in Central Asia had warm climates, and, therefore, the working conditions would be better, and more fresh fruit and vegetables would be available.

Mother looked at him and said, "Only God knows what will happen to us, but with Him it's only a one-way conversation." To Mother we were the downtrodden of the earth, being sent to God knows where and doomed forever to be strangers in a strange land.

People got onto the cars in an orderly way without any wrangling or complaints. Fortunately several other families in our boxcar also had children our age, which made the trip much more bearable for Hershel and me during what turned out to be an incredibly long journey. The rest of the passengers shuffled quietly into the middle of the car. They stood, huddled together, looked around, and began selecting their bunks. Father secured a corner place by the window, and Mother arranged our sleeping bunks.

When the train finally moved, the general impression was that it was heading south toward Moscow. Hershel and I sat on the top bunk and watched the beautiful sunset through the small window. As the pastureland disappeared from view, it gave way to the endless thick forest. The train traveled slowly, about 10 to 15 miles per hour, and the winding river followed the train track for some time until dusk set in.

We traveled evenings and nights as much as possible to avoid being bombed, but that wasn't always practical. Our first night on the train we made several short stops in small villages, but it was too dark to see anything. Besides, the sliding door on the car was locked from the outside at night because there were just a few guards with rifles who supervised the entire train.

During daytime the sliding door could be opened with permission. Mother was nagging Father about getting some milk for Velvel because she was still nursing him and her breast milk was drying up. Velvel was very thin and crying a lot. My father told Mother at the first train stop he would get some milk, but for now to give Velvel some cheese to suck on. Some of the other children in the car were also ill, so the place sounded like a nursery with all the crying.

Keeping Hershel at my side was my job, and he was a handful. But we and two other boys developed close friendships. Together we played checkers and other games that we made up throughout the journey.

The first longer stop came two days later at a railway junction somewhere between Leningrad and Moscow. The guards gave us permission to get off the train, but we were warned to stay close because when the whistle blew for the third time, the train would leave and those left behind would be stranded. Hershel and I learned to hold the teakettle near the train's idling engine to collect steam for tea.

The train was moved around from place to place, and most of the time we had no idea where we were. Early in the morning in one small town surrounded by a forest, our train was moved to the side rails. The locomotive was detached, and we were stranded there until evening. The boxcars were locked from the outside, and no one was permitted to get off. To everyone's relief, a new and much larger locomotive arrived and was attached to our train.

We traveled at night and in the morning stopped at a village, but no one was permitted to get off. While we were parked on the side rails, we could see German planes heading toward their targets, and we could hear constant bombardment. Later we realized that those planes were heading toward Leningrad. The battle of Leningrad was heating up, and the Germans were planning to capture the city.

What puzzled us was what we were doing there. Siberia, the Urals, and Central Asia were all in the opposite direction. People speculated that perhaps the Russians were moving us by back roads to avoid being bombed or that the main railway line was destroyed. No one could figure out what was happening from moment to moment.

During one short stopover, Father and Mother, with Velvel in her arms, got off the train, and I was left to keep an eye on Hershel. When the locative blew its first whistle, people started to run toward the train. Fortunately, Mother had already returned with milk for Velvel, and there was enough for Hershel and me. Father had the bread, some salami, and a bottle of vodka.

"To the train and wherever the hell it takes us"

Although Mother felt the vodka was a waste of their meager trading resources, it actually helped to break the ice with our neighbors occupying the bunk spaces to the left and right of us. Father introduced himself, his wife, and children to our neighbors. He then opened the bottle and poured a little vodka into each extended tin cup held by the three neighbors who came over.

One of them raised his cup and made a toast. "To the train and wherever the hell it takes us!" Just as they put the cup to their lips, the train moved with a strong jerk. They fell back and managed to swallow some of it, but the rest of it ended up on their faces. As they composed themselves, they looked at each other and started laughing out loud. This was the first and the last time such exuberant laughter was heard in our boxcar during the entire trip.

It was getting dark, but the explosions and flashes seemed to indicate we were moving toward the fighting rather than away from it. We could hear the whine of the German bombers as they dropped their bombs on a town not too far from us. During the night the train made several jerky stop-and-forward moves.

In the morning we were awakened by the guards as they opened the big sliding door. The first question to the guard was, "Where are we?"

In a loud voice the guard answered, "Welcome to Leningrad!" We were flabbergasted. What were we doing here? How were we going to get out?

As the Germans attempted to surround the city, there were few avenues for escape available. Did that mean that we would be in Leningrad for the duration of the war? No one really knew the answer to any of these questions. Besides, the Germans seemed to have been unstoppable up to that time, and no one believed that the Red Army had the means to stop them.

Before getting off the train in Leningrad, we were given our ration of bread and some black coffee. The guard said women and children would stay behind and help with the wounded. All able men would help fortify the defenses.

We were in Leningrad for about a month during the summer of 1941. It was a horrifying experience. Artillery bombarded the town at night. Our family stayed together right by the train the whole time.

The conditions in town were terrible. Food, water, and electricity were in short supply or rationed. There were dead bodies everywhere, not only from bombings, but also from starvation and disease. Many people ate rats in order to survive.

People were being evacuated by ferry from the city across Lake Ladoga to the mainland. I don't recall seeing any other form of transportation except for military trucks operating in the city at the time.

Those images are clear in my mind as though they happened yesterday. As to why we were there or, more importantly, how we got out, I am not sure. My time line indicates we were in Leningrad during the summer of 1941, and we got out before the siege of Leningrad in September 1941 began.

We again left by train from Leningrad and traveled by back roads to Vologda near Moscow, where we connected again with the Trans-Siberian Railway tracks that took us eastward across the vastness of Russia's Siberian land mass. We were anxious to get out of the war zone, but we were not the Russians' first priority. Of course, the war was.

Moving forward was a slow process; we were moved back and forth from one track to another. Most of the time it was to clear the track for troop and supply movement. Unbeknown to us, somehow as forced labor, we became part of the Soviets' greater war effort.

The Trans-Siberian Railway

The main route of the Trans-Siberian Railway runs from Moscow to Vladivostok. The rail line stretches more than 9,200 km (5,700 miles) and crosses seven time zones. Note that this is more than twice the distance from Los Angeles to New York. The railway was built between 1891 and 1916, under Tsar Alexander III, and including its connecting rail lines is the longest railway in the world. During WWII, the railway played several important roles. Some fortunate Jews were able to use it to escape Europe and find refuge in China and Japan. Germans made use of the railway to purchase and transport items essential to their war efforts from Japan. For the Soviets, the railway was used to evacuate entire factories and industries (including the largest producer of tanks) from western Russia to Siberia, after the Germans invaded Soviet territory in 1941.

6

BREAD OR DEATH

Survival on the train came down to two words: bread or death. Without the daily bread ration, death was a certainty. Our daily food portion generally consisted of a kettle of warm cabbage soup, orange in color, with carrots and other vegetables floating on top. Once in a great while we were even given potato soup with little bits of horse meat.

When the train stopped, the soldiers who guarded the train would bring the soup and the bread rations and distribute them daily—that is, most of the time. In addition, we were given a couple buckets of clean drinking water, which was not to be used for washing the face. The bread ration consisted of less than a pound of dark black bread for each adult and even less for children. The bread was heavy and had a hard crust with a soft mud-type consistency inside.

The daily bread and bowl of soup were barely enough to keep body and soul together. What sustained us was the bartering my parents did at station stops.

Given the desperate situation we found ourselves in, where we never had enough to eat and nothing was ever guaranteed, bartering was a necessary thing to do if we were to supplement our meager food rations and get the nutrition we needed. Not everyone was cut out to be a haggler. Luckily, my parents were.

To be an effective barterer you first of all had to speak the language, and my parents spoke Yiddish, Polish, and Russian. They would get off the train with some of the things they brought with them that had value—bowls, silverware, candle holders, tablecloths, bedding, jewelry. The silver they carried with them was in fact not real silver, but they sold and traded it as if it was.

The peasants in the villages did not have much themselves, so they desired anything that looked valuable or that looked as if it might have come from rich people or royalty.

My parents would introduce themselves with our predicament: "We're being shipped to Siberia, we don't have enough to eat." The peasants in those train-stop towns understood that because nobody had enough to eat. They were farmers selling their goods, and sometimes they really could have used those goods for themselves.

The bartering back and forth started with a conversation, something that you had in common. My father would ask whether they had pigeons and if he found out they did, he struck up a conversation. Another thing of course was vodka. He had vodka to trade. If a farmer had a horse, he would concoct tales of having raced horses.

To make a good trade my parents exaggerated some things about their items. If it was a tablecloth, they embellished its worth by saying it belonged to some prince and therefore it was very valuable. They would go on to say, "We would never have given it up except we have three children who are dying. We are willing to trade it for some food. God will bless you for your kindness." They knew how to get to people's emotions.

Sometimes Father would persuade people to trade with him by saying, "I have written down your name and this village's name, and I will come back to give you another bargain." In reality, he could not read or write and had no intention or means of ever returning.

In this kind of environment Mother and Father were both unrelenting in their effort to keep us all alive.

In addition to food, sanitation was also a problem. The toilet was reduced to a slit in the floor with practically no privacy, and washing up was done at train stops whenever possible. At night we could recognize each other by smell first and then by sight.

We also had to deal with the lice, which caused typhoid and other infectious diseases. I remember the stale, sour smell of sweat and urine and human waste. There was no privacy at all. It's amazing how important privacy is to people. Unless you have been without it, you do not understand.

In a small village east of the Volga River, the train stopped and Mother got off the train to barter for some milk. Just as the peasant woman poured the milk in Mother's cup, the final whistle blew. Mother covered the cup with her scarf and started running for the train. Father and another man started yelling at her, "Get rid of the milk! Get rid of the milk!" Mother did not listen, and then the train started moving.

When she reached the boxcar, she first put the milk gently on the floor and then tried to pull herself up. Our car was past the platform, so she had trouble reaching something to grab. Fortunately, the train was not yet at full speed, so Father and other men jumped off the train. They picked her up and threw her in the boxcar. Somehow the men managed to grab the sidebars of the sliding door, and with the help of others in the car, they were pulled in.

When Mother got up and lifted her cup to look at how much milk was left, a loud cheer came from the spectators. Father took out what was left of the vodka. He took a small sip and passed it on to the other people who had helped.

Mother's main concern was Velvel. He was ill and needed milk. Somehow she managed to always come back with some, and often she also had potatoes she would steal from a farmer's field. The war brought about food shortages and scarcities of just about everything except misery.

Precious Coal

These were coal-burning locomotives. Behind the locomotive was a car full of coal. At each station the train would take on more coal, and in the process of filling that car of coal and the fireman stoking that coal in the engine, some of the smaller pieces would fall to the ground around the tracks.

Everybody would jump off and go around scrounging to collect the coal in bags or in our pockets or in whatever we could find to put it in. The nuggets of coal we collected fit in the palm of my hand.

A couple of the older boys and I were given the responsibility of collecting coal by the rails when the train stopped at a larger station. Coal gathering was an important function because the weather in the Russian Siberian territories through which we would cross could be severe even in the fall. We needed to keep a fire in the stove in the boxcar going to heat water and milk bottles for the children and cook anything that could be gathered to make soup. Unfortunately, milk, meat, salami, and potatoes were luxuries, and there was a very short supply of those items.

Along the route the train would stop hundreds of times by villages, small and large towns, and sometimes in the middle of nowhere—as the days and weeks passed.

When the locomotive was unhitched from the train at the station, it was safe to get off. Sometimes the locomotive would detach for a short period of time just to take on coal and water, which was located on a track away from the station. In those circumstances it was dangerous to try to predict when the locomotive would be reattached. Sometimes the locomotive would be gone for a day or more, and sometimes it was back in twenty minutes.

Accidents were a common occurrence during our journey. An older boy from our boxcar went under the train tracks to collect some coal, and just as he slid across the track on his way back, the train moved, killing him instantly. I was devastated by this boy's death because he was my friend.

Unfortunately I don't recall his name, but his mother never did recover from the ordeal. The war had already taken her husband and two other children. When her boy was buried in a hurried shallow grave next to the rails, she said, "I give to this cursed land my first born. Now I have nothing worth living for!"

There were other instances where boys and adults from other boxcars had lost fingers, arms, and legs in a similar manner.

One time Hershel was underneath and going for a piece of coal, and I grabbed him by his feet and pulled him out just as the train started moving. He was battered and his legs scratched in that close call. Despite that near tragedy, other close scrapes, and that other boy losing his life, it did not stop us from continuing to collect coal.

Struggle for Survival

On the train, we Jews and non-Jews were cooped up in close quarters for weeks on end, having to share the same cramped space, breathe the same foul air, and be subjected to the same indignities and inconveniences. It is not as if all of the conflict and bad blood and anti-Semitism was forgotten, but the circumstances we found ourselves in together made us, at least for the duration of that experience, civil to each other.

The anti-Semitism and tension could also be temporarily put aside when someone had a bottle of vodka to share. Passing around some liquor, people talked and told each other about their lives in Poland and laughed at the same stupid jokes. A certain civility prevailed on those occasions.

Even so, the hatred and distrust that lay just under the surface never really left and would sometimes burst out. This was true with children too. Once, another boy and I went after a piece of coal and when I grabbed for it and got it away from him, he said, "You dirty Jew, you don't belong here." My reaction was to fight back.

The sharp division between Jew and Christian disappeared, and we pretended to be comrades in arms. For the rest of the journey, we were all Poles engaged in a common struggle for survival. Discussions among us were mainly about the good times before the war when there was plenty of food. Talk ranged from life on the farm, family ties, to work or business relationships, and the showing of family pictures.

There was also the recounting of horror stories about the sheer brutality of the German soldiers during the occupation when the war began. I remember these three:

A Polish woman on our train told us how one evening a squad car of four drunken German officers came to their farm and asked if they were hiding any Jews. She said no, but a Jewish woman, her baby, and husband were in fact hiding in a secret grain room under the barn. When the Jewish woman heard the soldiers getting close to where the family was hiding, she started breastfeeding the baby to keep him quiet. She then put a blanket around the baby and tightly pressed the baby to her breast. By the time the German soldiers finished their search and left, the baby had suffocated and died. The storyteller and her family fled to the Soviet side where they were arrested and ended up on our train.

A large Polish man with a scar on his face told us how the Germans stormed into his town near the German border and disarmed everyone. Then they rounded up the mayor, the chief of police, business leaders, the school principal, and other community leaders. Without saying a word, the Germans lined these leaders up against a wall and shot them dead. This storyteller was shot by a solider as he was running away, thus explaining the deep scar on his face. He made his way to the Soviet side of the border, but the Russians were going to send him back to Poland based on the Ribbentrop-Molotov Pact. He managed to bribe the NKVD official and promised to become a Communist. That's how he came to be on our train.

A Jewish woman in our boxcar sat in a corner all by herself and sang a Jewish lullaby over and over again. Everyone thought she was crazy, but her husband told us what made her so sad. Apparently when they were arrested by the

German soldiers in Lublin, a German officer grabbed her baby from her breast and threw the infant up in the air while another soldier bayoneted the child in midair. The sight of her baby being run through with a bayonet was beyond belief. The woman had been withdrawn ever since.

War Zone

As long as we were still in reach of the *Luftwaffe* bombers, traveling by train posed a danger. A Russian troop train on the tracks in front of us took a direct hit from a bomb dropped by a German plane. When we got off the train to look at what happened, we saw incredible destruction. It clearly reminded us that we were still in the war zone.

The locomotive was on its side, and steam and hot water were leaking out of the boiler. The tracks were twisted with human and horse bodies scattered everywhere. It was a terrible scene, but at least the wounded had already been taken to hospitals. We stood there stunned looking at the devastation. Then we heard a plane overhead, and without hesitation everyone made a dash to the ditch and wheat field beside the tracks.

We knew we still had a long journey before us. The Soviet Union was a very large country, and the war zone covered a vast territory. These German bombers' reach was beyond the war zone, and their targets were rail lines that carried war supplies for the military. But the Germans made no distinction between civilian and military targets. They bombed everything that moved.

When the conductor on our train heard an airplane engine overhead, he would stop the train and blow the locomotive whistle. That was a signal for everyone to get off the train and scatter. The safest destination would be to run toward the woods or grass field and wait until the all clear whistle signal was blown.

The Germans would bomb certain sections of the track, and the Russian crews would quickly fix them. In one instance, we arrived at a recently bombed station, and all the able men on our train were enlisted to help with the cleanup. We stayed there for three days. It was slow moving forward. It seemed that every time we moved forward in a certain direction for a couple days, all of a sudden in the morning we were right back where we started.

We kids played a lot of checkers on the train. We improvised a board and pieces. A couple people had decks of cards, but those were reserved for the adults.

My mother used to grab me and my brother and pull us close to her to sing to us. I have to admit she did not have much of a singing voice. She also told us stories about her childhood. She said that when she was a little girl she played with her doll. She told us about her sisters. She recounted how she and her siblings and friends used to play in the streets. She recalled working in the barn on the family farm. She told about a brother who was killed.

In our boxcar a woman who taught school back in Poland expressed a desire to teach us children. She grabbed any of us who would sit still long enough to listen to her. I was one of the few who did. I used to like those lessons. It was a dose of normalcy and routine amid the chaos.

So far during the journey, Mother and Father got along. They had a common goal, and that was survival. They cooperated in most things. Father would play with us children and tell us stories. Unfortunately, I don't remember any of them.

He had a roving eye, and once or twice Mother had to remind him that he had a family to take care of. He would say, "Haven't I been doing just that?"

And she would reply, "Yes, you have, but old habits of *fierman* are hard to shake," or something to that effect. It loses something in the translation from Yiddish to English.

After we departed from Leningrad we were on the train for about a month before we finally left the fighting behind us. The train had extended stops lasting several days at Perm, Sverdlovsk (Yekaterinburg), and Omsk. Of course, there were many stops in between because the towns are far apart from each other.

Somewhere between Omsk and Novosibirsk, at one of those stops in a small town, Father got off the train to barter for food.

At nightfall the whistle blew and everyone who had gotten off began to board the train— except my father.

Mother was frantic. She asked everyone in our boxcar returning to the train, "Have you seen Chaskiel?"

The answer was the same. The last time anyone had seen him was near a tavern arguing with a young woman. We had no idea what happened to him. Mother reasoned that he must have gotten drunk, started a ruckus, got hit over the head, and was lying in the street. She wanted to go and look for him, but what would she do with her babies?

I said that I would go look for him, but she said, "No, I need you to stay here and help me with Hershel." She was thinking of taking us with her while she looked for Father, but should the train leave, she would be stuck in the middle of nowhere.

She asked a friend to go and look for him. The friend went up and down the station and looked for Father in the tavern, but couldn't find him.

The tracks needed to be cleared for troop trains and armament that passed through heading for the front. The locomotive was moved from the front of the train to the back where it pushed the train to some empty tracks located at the back of the station and took off. We were parked there without the locomotive all night, but my father was gone and nowhere to be found. When the locomotive was reconnected to the train, there was no getting off because the train was being moved around from track to track, and no one knew what was happening.

Finally the train took off and kept on going. Mother, Hershel, Velvel, and I were stranded on the train. Even worse, Father had with him all our passports, the precious food ration cards, and all the money. Without them, we became dependent for survival entirely on our neighbors, who themselves had little food to spare.

After my father abandoned us, my mother spoke of him as though he were dead. When asked what happened to him she would say, "My husband got off the train and was killed," but of course she could not explain how.

As for me, I did not think for a minute he could get killed that easily. I am sure my mother thought he simply ran off with another woman but told others he was killed.

In Novosibirsk the train changed direction and headed south on the Turkestan-Siberian railway (Turk-Sib) line, and at Bamaul we crossed to Kazakhstan, which is located in Central Asia.

We were hitting drier and sunnier weather. In Almaty, the former capital of Kazakhstan, the locomotive was detached from our train so the locomotive could take on water and coal. Somehow the locomotive got into an accident with a freight train and was disabled. Thus, we were parked there on side rails for over a week. It was the first time during the journey that people had an opportunity to wash up and wash their clothes. It was such a refreshing experience that words can't quite explain the liberating sensation. The next day we could no longer recognize each other by smell.

The rest of the journey through Kazakhstan was long and arduous. We did leave the fighting behind us, but not the war. Food was in short supply, and people helped as much as they could, but it wasn't enough. The Russians would not issue us new ration cards, thinking we were cheating. Mother was a proud, self-sufficient woman who, in desperation, became a beggar.

At the larger city station stops, Mother would sometimes attempt to beg for food from farmers who were selling their produce to people on the trains. But she wasn't very good at it. She thought it was a degrading act.

She would hold Velvel in her arms and cover him with a blanket. Hershel and I were at her side. Then she would put out her hand and try to look pitiful and beg. The problem was that everyone on the train looked pitiful.

I remember one time a Russian woman gave her a few kopecks and looking at her up and down she said to my mother, "You poor creature, you," and my mother took that money and threw it away, muttering, "I'm not a poor creature." She would not give in to self-pity or self-degradation. She would not be humiliated that way. She said, "It's better that we starve than become beggars."

Our main support and help came from the people on the train, and often the Russian guards gave us our share of the rations without asking for our ration cards as we stood in line with others waiting for food. If we didn't produce the cards, some guards would occasionally motion us, "Out of the line."

Nothing to Live For

A Polish woman in our boxcar who had befriended Mother also had bad luck ever since she left Poland. Her husband had died in Arkhangelsk. Her older boy was the one killed under the train while collecting coal. Mother was very sympathetic to her and helped to take care of her baby while this woman was stricken with grief. The shock of her older son's death never left her.

Before burying her son, the distraught woman came to my mother to thank her for her kindness during the dark days after her son's death in the accident. Before Mother could reply, the woman said she admired Mother for not giving up after her husband disappeared from the train.

A month later, in the middle of the night, the woman maneuvered near us. She touched my head and she hugged both Hershel and me. Then she said, "You take care of your mother. Be kind to her."

She was clutching her dead baby who had died of typhus.

She handed my mother her passport and three ration cards, saying, "Your name is now … (I do not remember her name). The Russians won't be able to tell us apart. Use these ration cards for the children and yourself, but use them sparingly because if the guards find out, they will throw you in jail. I won't need them anymore."

She then opened the sliding door of the boxcar as the train was moving. Our train was curving around a bend, and another train was coming from the opposite direction. Before anyone could react, she slid the door open, letting in a shaft of light from the oncoming train's headlights. She grabbed her dead baby, said, "I have nothing to live for," and jumped.

We heard the other train rushing by with great force. For a long time that noise haunted me. My mother could not stop crying. She pulled me close to her and said, "Remember this woman because she might have just saved our lives."

Although death was not a stranger to any of us, this single act by this poor, sad woman giving up on life in that way unhinged many of us. We used this woman's ration cards almost to the end of the trip until someone reported us. Although the guard took the ration cards away from us, they kept on giving us the rations that saved our lives.

During the entire experience of the war, people were dying on the streets. People were dying on the train and in accidents off the train. Some people committed suicide. Some were shot. Death was not a stranger. We did not think about survival per se, we just thought from moment to moment about what we had to do next to remain among the living. We were looking for reasons to live, and my mother reinforced repeatedly my reason to live. Through her bravery alone she would do things that were dangerous in the Soviet Union, such as stealing. Stealing was dangerous business there, but she didn't care. She took the risk.

From the time we left Arkhangelsk to the time we arrived in Samarkand, including the week we spent in Tashkent waiting for a clear track, almost three months had passed.

During that time we covered a distance of 7,340 kilometers (4,550 miles). It's hard to comprehend the incredible distances we covered, until you look at the map of the former Soviet Union. We traveled nearly twice the distance across the United States from New York to Los Angeles.

Leaving Arkhangelsk, we passed again through Leningrad in the summer of 1941. After being forced to spend a horrifying month there helping with the war effort, we were ordered back on the Trans-Siberian Railway and, for the next two months, with much hunger and death along the way, reached our destination of Samarkand, Uzbekistan. We later learned that this trip from Arkhangelsk to Samarkand should have taken only 3 weeks.

7

WELCOME TO THE JEWEL OF THE ORIENT: SAMARKAND

"Welcome to Samarkand, the jewel of the Orient! Take everything with you because you will not be coming back to the train," a tall military officer shouted as our train pulled into Samarkand station. It was a pleasant fall day in 1941 when the large sliding door on the boxcar opened for the last time to let us out.

On the ground we were lined up in a straight line in front of the train. The officer was a tall, good-looking blonde young man. He wore a new shiny uniform, and his chest was covered with medals. A group of NKVD officials dressed in civilian clothes followed the officer as he went from boxcar to boxcar. He assigned an NKVD official to each boxcar so he could check the names of passengers on the ground against the original lists.

The NKVD took a new census of the survivors and recorded the names of those who had died or disappeared. Mother was holding Velvel and crying loudly. Hershel and I were standing next to Mother and also crying. The young officer came over and asked Mother why she was crying. She showed the officer the blanket with Velvel wrapped in it and told the officer that Velvel had died that day on the train.

He asked one of the women officials to take the baby and tag him. He further emphasized that on the tag she should include name of the child, mother's name, train number, and date of death. The officer then asked Mother, "What is your name?"

She quietly said, "My name is Fajga Dawidowicz. These are my other sons, Mendel and Hershel," and then she handed the blanket with Velvel to the woman.

The officer said, "I am sorry, but the war is hard on everyone." He gave Mother a receipt for Velvel, told her to talk to the nurse in the warehouse across the tracks and said she would help Mother with her son's burial. "Do you have your papers handy?" he asked.

She said, "No! My husband got off the train near Novosibirsk and had all of our papers with him. The train left, and we don't know what happened to him."

The officer said, "After you get settled, come and see me in the police station in town, and we will get you new papers." He handed her a pass so she could leave the group and come to see him.

After the census taking was completed, we crossed the tracks, with each boxcar's passengers kept together as a group. On the other side of the rail yard was a big open empty field, and adjacent to the track stood an old warehouse with several offices located inside. When we walked in we saw six long tables with Russian-, Polish-, and Yiddish-speaking women behind them ready to register the people from the train.

Mother was approached by the nurse who had taken Velvel and said, "Tomorrow morning we will find a nice spot for you to bury your son." The nurse gave Mother a slip that told her where and when Velvel would be buried. Mother told the nurse she couldn't read Russian, so the nurse said, "I can write it in Polish."

Well, Mother said, "I can't read Polish either."

Then the nurse said, "I can't write Jewish."

Mother was relieved, because she didn't have to embarrass herself further by acknowledging that she can't even read Yiddish. So the nurse took her outside and pointed to the fence that surrounded the cemetery across the road. "You see that white building on the hill? Be there at 9 a.m., show them the slip, and they will show you where your son will be buried."

"But who will say *Kaddish* for my poor Velvel?" Mother thought out loud. The nurse told mother, "After the funeral we will find a Rabbi to say *Kaddish*, and at the appropriate time we will put up a stone for him." With her slip in hand, Mother grabbed Hershel and me close to her in a big hug. Then she quietly said, "We now have to be strong because this is all the family we have in this place."

Officially we were prisoners of the Soviet Union until June 22, 1941, when the Germans attacked the Soviet Union in Operation Barbarossa. The Soviets then made a pact with the Poles because they had the Polish Army under their occupation. No matter our status now, we were off the train in a foreign land with dwindling few possessions, and family was more important now than ever.

After the registration process was over, the officer called us all to attention. Then in a gentle, but firm, voice said to the group, "This year the collective farm to which you all have been assigned had a large harvest of cotton. All personnel, excluding some pregnant women and children, will be assigned to work in a factory that processes cotton."

The officer added that Polish prisoners were granted special status. "That means that you will not be interned, but you will be required to report to the police station at least once a month." We were to report any deaths and changes in home address or workplace. We were given two vouchers, one for housing and the other one for one blanket per person.

"The housing," he went on, "will be assigned to you when you get your work assignment. While we are getting all this sorted out, you will have to find a sleeping spot outside beneath the stars next to the warehouse. When you go to retrieve the blankets, you can thank me," the army officer said proudly. "I saved these blankets for my Polish prisoners. It is the first time a shipment of blankets was received in my region, and it will probably be the last. After you are finished processing, there will be potato soup and bread waiting for you."

A Note on Samarkand

When Uzbekistan was established in 1924, Samarkand, the second largest city, was the original capital. In 1930 the capital moved to the largest city, Tashkent. Samarkand is located at the crossroads of two of the many routes that became known as the Silk Road connecting China with Central Asia. Because of these routes, Samarkand became an important city and today is still the second largest city with a population of 700,000.

> *Jewish life in Samarkand between 1898 and 1917 was relatively stable, with many laws restricting Jews lifted. Thirty synagogues existed in Samarkand in 1917. The Bolshevik Revolution in 1917 forbade the practice of religion. By 1935 only one synagogue remained.*

The old cemetery across the street had a section designated for newcomers. When we got to the burial grounds, the corpses were already in the ground and the graves covered up. Two Jewish women and we were the only mourners there to attend the funeral, but we were all late, and no one could tell us where the bodies were buried. One of the workers was at least kind enough to tell us they had dug many graves for the Poles who arrived dead on the train in the last few days. He also said some of them were buried in mass graves.

He pointed Mother to one grave where children were buried, but the authorities did not provide them with any names. We really didn't know for sure where Velvel was buried or even if this was the right cemetery.

The two Jewish women were elderly sisters from the city of Lodz, and one of them had just buried her husband. Besides each other, the sisters had no other relatives or friends in Samarkand either. Together we five lost souls set up our camp close to the warehouse in that open field.

At night we all huddled together and shared the blankets and our body heat. With our empty, rumbling stomachs, we lay down under all the covers we could muster and enjoyed a panoramic view of the Samarkand clear sky full of bright stars. Hershel and I tried to count the stars until we fell asleep.

Cotton Picking

We slept in the field under the stars for over a week and later found refuge in the warehouse. The warehouse had a covered staircase leading to a loft. Under the stairs firewood was stored so we moved in there for the last couple of days.

Mother had trouble sleeping. She was concerned about what she would do with Hershel and me should she be assigned to a difficult work detail. Several days following the cemetery fiasco, we were instructed to go to the central police station for final registration and job assignment. We arrived at the police station loaded down with all our belongings.

A young Russian woman showed us where to put our bundles and told us to wait for Comrade Evan, the Commandant of the police station. We recognized him. He was the tall, blonde Russian officer who gave us the instructions in the warehouse. He started off by asking Hershel and me some questions about our father and about the trip. Then he said to Mother, "Your children speak Russian quite well."

She replied, "Young minds pick up everything easily."

"All right. Tell me why you used the dead woman's ration cards?"

"To save my children's lives," she answered. "Unfortunately I couldn't do much for my youngest."

"So you bribed the guard and split the rations with him," the officer accused her.

"No! No! There were no bribes!"

"Why didn't you report and ask them to issue you new ration cards?"

She said, "I did often, but they said that they couldn't issue us new ration cards without our passports."

"Typical bureaucrats!" he replied. "Now tell me what really happened to your husband."

So she told him again what she said at the train station, that my father had left the train. The Commandant's secretary, a young woman, wrote down every word Mother said. The secretary then read the words back to Mother and asked her if they were correct. After Mother said, "Yes," the secretary asked Mother to sign the paper. Mother put an X where her signature should go and told the officer, "I don't know how to sign my name."

Following the interrogation we were issued identification passports and permanent ration cards. Mother was then assigned to work in a large cotton-gin mill located on the outskirts of the city. Before we boarded the truck taking us to the cotton-gin mill, Mother asked the officer, "What will I do with my children when I work?"

"Take them with you," the officer replied, "They will tell you what to do with them."

"What about housing?" she asked.

"The workplace will find you a place to stay close to the cotton mill where you work," he assured her.

Uzbekistan had huge cotton and tobacco *kolhoz* (collective farms). After these commodities were harvested, they were bundled up and sent to the various locations in the city to be processed. Some people from the train were assigned to the cotton-processing industry and others to the tobacco plants.

The hardest part of processing the cotton was extracting the seeds from the raw cotton, which at that time was all done by hand. Large piles of raw cotton were piled on the ground, and workers sat on wooden benches hand picking the individual seeds from the cotton. For ten hours a day, six days a week, the laborers did this grueling work. The handpicked seeds were turned into oil.

The cotton was washed and made ready for the mills. The cotton industry required a large labor force. All able men were drafted into the army, so the Russians needed workers to take their place. The labor pool imported from Poland to work in the cotton industry helped supplement the Russian labor shortage. One really needed to have a job to survive in Samarkand at that time. The place of work determined your status, your residence, your food rations, and other necessities of life.

We waited on the truck in back of the police station until more people were processed and the truck filled up. The two Jewish sisters were also on the truck taking us to the cotton mill. At the entrance of the complex we were greeted by a couple of guards who told us to disembark. One of the guards pointed in the direction of a small, square brick building and instructed us to put our belongings inside. He assured everyone that their belongings would be safe there for the time being. This small building had two thick wooden doors fastened with a sliding metal latch and secured with a padlock.

After we placed our belongings there, we were ushered into a cafeteria and given some black bread and potato soup. We were all very hungry, so we attacked the food as if it was the best gourmet meal. After we finished eating, the guard introduced a short, skinny young woman, and said she was a kindergarten teacher. Then the guard introduced an Uzbek-looking man and said he was the manager of the mill. He had hard Asian features and darker olive skin. He wore loose clothing and a turban on his head.

The guard said, "Comrade Manager will assign all of you to workstations and show you how to do your jobs. While he is giving you instructions, Comrade Teacher will entertain your children and teach them Russian."

After the orientations, which took several hours, a guard led Mother and the sisters to pick up their belongings. From there we all went to our assigned lodging. The five of us were given a small mud hut with just one room and no amenities. There was a small table with three chairs, and in the corner was a small stove with some coal left over from the previous owner. The room had a dirt floor and two small windows with bars; one window was facing east and the other west.

While Mother worked, Hershel and I, and about twenty other children, were placed in the hands of Comrade Teacher. The work was hard for Mother. Raw cotton feels like sandpaper on your skin, and those seeds don't want to come out. The seeds had side effects causing her to develop inflamed eyes and a skin rash, and made her night blindness worse.

Right from the beginning Mother knew she had to get out of the cotton mill not only for her sake, but also because she was unhappy about how Hershel and I were treated. I was constantly getting into fights because the other children would pick on Hershel, and I would respond. The mill was not far from the bazaar, so sometimes I would grab Hershel and we would sneak out of the compound and wander around in the bazaar.

Peasants set up stalls on each side of a narrow walkway to form the open-air bazaar or marketplace. Covers overhead protected the area from the blazing sun. In the stalls, merchants would sell everything from live chickens to colorful clothing. Sometimes sellers would simply lay blankets on the ground to display the freshly picked produce they had brought in on their camels or donkeys.

Not only was Mother reprimanded when we were apprehended, but she was fearful we would be kidnapped by Tatars and sold into slavery. Stories of kidnappings and even cannibalism were circulating wildly. The authorities blamed all criminal activities on the Tatars, but in actuality the criminals were all locals.

Mother worked in the cotton mill for about six months, and during that entire time my fighting was a source of concern to her.

Tatars, also known as Tartars, are an ethnic group of people living in Eastern Europe and Northern Asia. The people were generally Asian looking, stocky with dark hair. The men often had a distinctive mustache.

A Model for Propaganda

In summer of 1942, a Russian film crew was making a propaganda film depicting Polish workers in the cotton industry "voluntarily" joining the war effort. The film showed the many ways cotton products were used by the Red Army to help them in the battle against the Nazis. The slogan was, "Polish workers help Red Army free their homeland."

During the film shooting, several people who appeared in the film were selected to be models for the posters advertising the film, and Mother with her dark exotic good looks was selected as one of the models. She was a bundle of energy with an intensity about her that could be appealing or intimidating depending on the situation.

The art studio was located in what is now Universitet, Bulvari, then considered to be the "cultural center." After the posters were finished, Mother was asked to stay on. The artist in the center liked to use her as a model for select students who were engaged in a project to portray the different faces of Samarkand during the war. Mother had the right complexion and features that could pass as both Asian and European.

I got to see her pose because she would take us with her, and it was such a departure from the factory and farm work she normally did. Where her previous jobs involved much physical labor and coming home sweaty and dirty and exhausted after standing on her feet all day, this was like a vacation by comparison.

She would sit on a chair or bench, or sometimes they put her on a donkey, in front of six or seven students who stood before canvases on easels painting in oils with brushes. She would often pose in costumes, one time as a Polish folk dancer, another time as a Russian folk dancer, and so on.

She was for all practical purposes a model during those sessions and for once she was being treated with at least a measure of dignity and appreciation. In those classes she was able to express something of her individuality and humanity. She was finally more than just a strong back.

8

BULLIES, BATTLES, AND BARTERING

In fall of 1942 the *zetskiy-sadik* (kindergarten in Russian) run by the art center had an opening. Many of the artists and university faculty's children attended that *zetskiy-sadik*. The children came from a diverse group of people: Russians, Poles, Uzbeks, and others. I was almost six, and Hershel was a year younger. I could get in, but Hershel's age was problematic. He was too young.

Through bribes, I'm sure, Mother managed to get us both enrolled. The place was more like a "children's home" than simply a kindergarten. We actually ate all our meals there and slept there, except for the weekends when we came home to stay with Mother.

The facility was quite large and housed about one hundred fifty children ranging in ages from four to eight. Mother's modeling studio was located about a mile from the kindergarten, and she lived an equal distance in the opposite direction. The property was sandwiched in between an administrative office building on the north side of the property and a busy road on the south side. A mesh fence enclosed all four sides of the property.

A three-floor, concrete building of typical Russian construction housed the *zetskiy-sadik* and was situated in the back of the property. The entrance gate was the only way to get in or out, and an armed guard sat in a small shed at the entrance. At night the gate was locked from the inside. A wide dirt road of about 50 yards in length led directly from the gate to the main building. Children playing in front of the building could be seen from the street.

The place was spartan and disorganized but nicer than what we were used to. Hershel and I had our own beds next to each other with a coarse horse blanket and maybe a pillow. Food rations were inadequate but better than in the cotton mill. We were even given warm jackets and shoes. Lice, hunger, and disease were the big killers of children in the facility. In summer mosquitoes and flies added to the discomfort.

In the morning there was organized activity for the children. After lunch the children were required to lie down to nap for an hour on a blanket in the classroom. Then it was out to the playground.

The superintendent of the *zetskiy-sadik* was a short, stocky man. His face was scarred from the disease of smallpox, which he had as a child. His name was Vladimir, and he ran the kindergarten like a dictator. Everyone except Mother was scared of him. She feared no one who was susceptible to a bribe, and in Samarkand that included almost everyone. Vladimir wouldn't hesitate to expel any child who was a troublemaker, but he could be lenient if the parents could make it worthwhile for him.

Mother somehow always managed to meet with Comrade Vladimir and our teachers on her trips to see us. Her bribes with money and the extra food she brought with her really sustained us. Mother's help went only so far, because it did not extend to the playground.

In the morning Hershel and I had different teachers, but in the afternoon we were in the same indoctrination classes. On the playground the kids would segregate themselves by nationalities. By appearance and language we fit in with both the Russian and Polish kids. In fact, we didn't look much different from the other boys except for the Asian children. We could speak both Russian and Polish so we mixed with both groups. The other Polish kids could also speak Russian, but among themselves they spoke Polish, which irritated the Russian kids. Of course, the teachers insisted we all speak Russian.

Hershel and I would speak Russian, but with Mother we would speak Yiddish. Tension broke out between the Polish and Russian kids over the language issue. Hershel and I were caught in the middle. The Polish kids wanted us to join them in their patriotic protest and speak Polish to annoy the Russians. We just wanted to be left alone and not get involved with either side, but that was not possible.

The ringleader of the Polish boys was a tall, loudmouthed kid. He would set the tone for the others to follow. This boy was slightly older than I, and one day he grabbed a piece of Hershel's bread ration right in front of me. I grabbed a small rock in my hand went up to this boy and told him to give the bread back to my brother.

The boy said, "No!" Then he taunted me and said, "What are you going to do about it, if I don't?"

Before he could say another word, I hit him as hard as I could with the stone along the side of his ear. The boy fell down and was bleeding, and the other boys ran away to get a teacher. A Russian boy by the name of Uri was standing there observing the fight.

Uri came up to me and said, "I have seen the whole thing and I will tell Vladimir that the Poles started the fight."

When the teacher came over, the bleeding boy was taken to the nurse. Hershel, Uri, and I were taken before Vladimir and told him our side of what happened. Uri was a very good witness. He embellished a little about the anti-Soviet attitude of the other Polish boys. After that, Uri and I became best friends.

Vladimir wanted to expel Hershel and me, but Mother had a price to pay in order to keep us in the school. After that incident Hershel and I were mostly left alone, but Mother knew the next time I got into a serious fight we would be thrown out. Eventually the incident was forgotten, and the Polish boys gave up their boycott of Russians.

Uri and I were involved in several fights with other bullies who picked on Hershel. Uri would come to my aid if the bully who started the fight was much bigger or when there were more than one of them. I, too, would come to Uri's aid when he needed help.

After a while a code developed on the playground. The other kids knew that if they picked on Hershel, there would a confrontation with Uri and me, and if one of us got a bloody nose, they wouldn't report it. Mother was always concerned that we would be thrown out. Fortunately, a new group of boys with serious mental problems was admitted and kept Vladimir and the teachers busy, so we went unobserved.

Survival at that time was an everyday struggle in Samarkand. People would die and lie in the street for several days before being removed. Any usable clothing would be stripped off the body. The corpse would be left lying there while people looked away or just stepped over it.

Stealing from work and bribery were a way of life in Samarkand, and Mother was quite good at both. In kindergarten we had to fight for everything, every bit of food, clothing, or medical attention. All employees in the facility were engaged in stealing on some level.

In addition to stealing food from the children, the employees of the kindergarten were always open to a bribe. The small bribes Mother brought for Vladimir and our teachers insured that Hershel's and my rations were not stolen or tampered with. She took care of the guard at the gate who kept an eye on the playground to make sure I was safe.

One time a bully, several years older than I, wanted the apple I was eating. I refused, so he punched me and gave me a bloody nose. I started to fight back, but the bully was getting the better of me. The guard at the gate saw the fight and rushed over and pulled the bully off me. He then told the bully to stay away from me or there would be consequences. The guard kicked the bully in the rear, and as the bully was running away, the bully scooped up the apple I had dropped on the ground and kept on going.

On weekends and holidays Mother would come to the school and take Hershel and me home with her. Hershel was frail, so he would slow us down when we walked to Mother's apartment. None of us was particularly full of energy, but sometimes Mother and I would take turns carrying Hershel. He loved it when Mother put him on my back and she walked next to me holding him up from the rear.

In her room, Mother would always find an exotic hiding place for money or food. She always had something for us to eat, but I am sure that sometimes the food she saved for us came from her own daily rations. I recall one time when she came to get us, Mother was brimming with pride. It was apparent that she had something special saved for us. In her room she had a hiding place under the stove. When she went to get her package, the rats had eaten not only the bread and salami, but also the money she kept there.

Mother's modeling job was more prestigious and meant a slight increase in food rations and a better place to live. Yet when that work ended, she was supposed to return to the cotton mill. Instead, she managed to get a doctor to give her a certificate saying she was allergic to cotton and transfer her to the tobacco factory. She knew that work in the tobacco factory was much harder. But tobacco was more rewarding in terms of giving her something valuable to bargain with. It turned out to be the thing that sustained us during the war because she used stolen tobacco to get us extra food and preferred treatment.

Until Mother started working in the tobacco plant, she had little to barter with for extra food. The war put a strain on all resources. Extra bread, coffee, meat, and cigarettes came with a very large premium. You could purchase many of these products in the bazaar or on the black market. In fact, there was no difference between the bazaar and the black market. The authorities were prone to bribes, so they tolerated black market activities.

"What have I done to deserve this?"

Hershel and I caught a good share of the diseases: measles, whooping cough, typhoid, and diphtheria, and we survived them all. Again Mother did her magic. She was able to bribe the doctors who controlled the scarce medication, and we survived. Then in the spring of 1943 Hershel came down with malaria and suffered with it for over a month.

In spite of every effort made by Mother and her doctor, Hershel died from that horrible disease. Mother and I were devastated. She grabbed me and held me tight to her bosom and said, "I will not let that happen to you." Then she looked up with her hands outstretched and shouted, "God in heaven, what have I done to deserve this?"

I don't recall her ever again talking to God in such an earnest way. She was raised in an observant home and kept a kosher home whenever possible, but on that day her faith was shaken. I too wanted to die. Hershel was my shadow. He was always next to me from the moment he started walking. I was his older brother, and during this entire trip I felt he was mainly my personal responsibility. Even when I got beaten up in a fight, I felt it was worth it because I did it for my younger brother. He was only a year younger, yet I had that overriding responsibility of an older brother that if I didn't protect him, no one would. In my mind he remained my shadow for a long time after he was gone.

Something Special to Eat

Mother's work in the tobacco factory was physically hard. After the harvest, the tobacco leaves were dried in the sun. Afterward, the dry leaves were collected and brought to the factory to be turned into tobacco. The tobacco went through several other procedures before being shipped to manufacturers who made cigarettes and cigars.

At the tobacco factory Mother met Haia, a young single Jewish woman from Szestochowa, Poland. When the

Germans occupied the city, Haia's husband and two children were murdered by her Polish neighbors. Haia and her cousin escaped to Bialystok. There the Russians arrested them and deported them to Arkhangelsk. Haia's cousin enlisted in the Red Army after the German invasion of the Soviet Union. She had been deported to Samarkand on an earlier train. She managed to avoid Leningrad, coming directly to Samarkand, and had been assigned to her current job ever since.

She had a small mud house located across the street from the cemetery where Velvel was buried. Haia asked Mother to move in with her, fearing that the authorities may move in someone else she couldn't trust. Mother accepted her offer, and from then on they became partners in crime.

The tobacco factory job and Haia were a godsend to Mother. Together they devised a scheme to steal small quantities of tobacco and share the loot with the foreman and the guards. It was risky, but Mother felt that without her ability to bribe Vladimir and others to obtain more food, she and I would perish anyway.

Shortly after Mother started, she came to visit me regularly in the middle of the week and looked happy. She brought me *kisloye-moloko* (sour milk, buttermilk). It was delicious and nutritious beyond description. As usual, she also shared some of it with Vladimir, my teacher, and the guard. I would always save some for Uri, who became my best friend after Hershel died. On weekends we walked to the house shared by Mother and Haia. They always had something special for me to eat.

Haia was an educated woman. She could read and write in Polish, Russian, German, and Yiddish. She read in a Polish paper that the Polish Delegatura had set up one hundred thirty-nine orphanages for refugee children, including some especially for Jewish children. Some of these homes for Polish orphans and semi-orphans had been set up in Samarkand, Tashkent, and other cities in Central Asia. Enrollments were open to children of Polish citizens who had been deported by the Russians after the start of the war, and some orphanages, she read, were supported by a Joint Distribution Committee in America.

9

WE THREE MUSKETEERS

Mother had no idea who this American Joint Distribution Committee was, nor did she care. According to the article, the orphan children's home was set up for children of Polish parents. It was for both Jewish and non-Jewish children who had lost one or both parents to the Nazis.

After hearing about the place Mother and Haia went to check it out. It was a long walk from their home in the city. They had to cross the tracks and go east past the bazaar and tobacco factory to the edge of the city. From there they walked on the Black Road, known from ancient days as a road full of bandits.

Unlike the fabled Silk Road dating to ancient times, the Black Road meandered along as cobblestones in the city and later as dirt for perhaps twenty miles up into the mountains where it was reputed that the bandits hid out.

The last mile on the dirt Black Road before the children's home was marked by a rice-processing factory. The rice factory was built on the outskirts of Samarkand on a stream that ran parallel with the road. It was a pleasant walk, that last mile from the rice factory to the children's home. The stream was on the left as you walked from town to the children's home. The water was clean, and on the left bank was a fenced-off orchard with all kinds of fruit.

Hugging the fence were big "uruk" trees with their branches extending over the stream. They produced a sweet fruit that looked just like a white and then reddish blackberry as it ripened. It must have been about two miles from Mother's home to the tobacco factory and another eight miles to the children's home.

The complex consisted of three long, single-floor concrete buildings arranged in a square with one side open. The middle building faced the Black Road. The entrance was located in the center of the middle building, and it could be seen from the Black Road. A large square courtyard filled the open space among the three buildings.

The center building housed the administration office, kitchen, cafeteria, supplies, and sleeping quarters for the administrative staff. The building on the right side housed the older children and functioned as a school. The building on the left housed the younger children and had a kindergarten. None of the buildings were connected to each other. Each building had to be locked separately at night.

No modern amenities such as electricity or running water existed. The water was carried with a bucket by hand from the stream located across the Black Road. The outhouses were a proper distance behind the center building and had to be relocated from time to time. The property had no fence or gate. Uzbeks, who took their products to the bazaar by donkeys, would often cross our property in front of the center building.

David, the superintendent of the Polish project, was a tall, very thin man with a large forehead and hooked nose. He was responsible for getting the Polish children's home established. He spoke all the languages including Uzbek. His hair was always in his eyes, and when you spoke to him, you had the feeling he looked right through you. He didn't seem to be interested in mundane daily activities. He focused on keeping the facility within the Polish culture until the end of the war.

The children's home housed about three hundred children, and most of them were Jewish. Half the kids were classified as orphans. They did not know whether any of their relatives were alive. Those who knew their parents were alive had somehow been separated from them. The reason given for a special, separate Polish children's home was to educate the children in Polish culture so they could successfully be reunited with their families after the war was over. That was partially true. The actual purpose was to indoctrinate the children into a Polish culture that was compatible with Soviet ideology.

As soon as Mother and Haia came back from their inspection, they started to plan how to get me enrolled in this Polish children's home. The problem was that I wasn't quite an orphan, so I received closer scrutiny than true orphans did. To Mother obstacles like that were no problem. She now had tobacco, a currency to bargain with. Mother was capable of bribing Stalin himself in order to get me in. Needless to say, she succeeded.

At first I didn't want to be there because I had my friend Uri, and together we ruled the roost in the kindergarten school. Mother tried to bribe me with some candy to get me to stay for a couple of weeks just to see if I liked it. I didn't like the Polish children's home, and after being there for two weeks, I ran away. I met up with Uri in the Russian kindergarten. We broke out and together spent the day in the bazaar stealing some apples.

When we got caught by the bazaar policeman, he sent for my mother. Fajga Dawidowicz was already known among the bribe-takers, and when she saw me in the police station, she was shaken. "Are you all right?" she repeated several times.

I gave her a flippant answer, "You don't have to worry about me! I can take care of myself."

Without warning or hesitation, Mother slapped me across the face as hard as she could. She caught me by surprise and almost knocked me off my feet. I had never seen her that mad. She grabbed me and shook me several times. Then she looked into my eyes and said, "You are all I have left, and I am trying very hard to keep you alive. Do you have any idea what I had to do to get you enrolled in that children's home?"

Mother gave the policemen some tobacco right in front of me. I don't know whether it was for calling her or whether it was to put a scare into me. That policeman was a huge man. He grabbed me by my collar, dragged me to where the jail cells were located, and said to me, "Do you see these criminals? They are going to Siberia. Do you want to go with them or do you want to go back to the children's home?"

That did it. I went with Mother. This was the first time and, to the best of my recollection, the last time Mother ever slapped me.

Before letting me go, the policemen added, "The next time we catch you stealing in the bazaar, you will be sent to Siberia!" I was more scared of what being sent to Siberia would do to my Mother than what it would do to me. The fear and anger in Mother's eyes that day stayed with me always.

Our Daily Bread

During the next few years I spent in that children's home, I grew up and became self-sufficient. Mother came to visit me less frequently because the distance and the danger on the Black Road were difficult for her—and I was to find out later, for us all. She always tried to get someone to come with her or get a ride.

Mother's visits to the children's home affected the other children whose parents rarely visited. So she tried to bring something for them as well, at least for those who were my friends. When she came, she would always bring some food. It was usually *kisloye-moloko* (sour milk, buttermilk). Sometimes it included a piece of salami sandwiched between two crusty *garbushkas* (end pieces or the heels) of bread.

The bread we received daily was very black. It had a crusty exterior and a soft mushy interior. A slice of bread was always desirable, but if that slice were the garbushka, that made it a treat. If you were fortunate enough to have some garlic and rub it on the garbushka crust, that would make the black bread taste incredible. Of course, as a rare treat, eating the bread with salami would drive my taste buds crazy.

The ration card specified that each child was entitled to about two slices of bread three times a day. The bread was carefully sliced and weighed and placed on a round tin plate next to a bowl of potato soup, rice *potage* (broth), or some other warm concoction that came with that meal. Once in a great while, especially when we had dignitaries visit, some meat would find its way into the soup.

The food was inadequate for growing children to thrive or survive. In the children's home, the less resourceful kids or those with no outside help would be the first to die. During the war years, life for most people was a daily struggle for survival. Children were the first to be affected by the cold, malnutrition, diseases, and abuse. Life was at the most primitive stage. Only the strong and most determined survived.

One boy I knew named Edmund was being bullied by a couple kids who wanted him to give up his bread, and he called out, "Mendel, I need your help."

In that moment Edmund looked to me just like Hershel. It made me want to protect him. I said to another rough-and-tumble boy I'd met, Pioter, "Let's go in there," and we got into a very serious fight. All of us got bloody, but these bullies walked away knowing we were not to be messed with.

One of the kids looked back and said, "Are you guys like the Three Musketeers?" and liking the image that evoked we said, "Yes, we are."

From that moment on we made it clear that anybody who messed with one of us had to deal with all three of us. We made a commitment to each other right then and there. We sort of became blood brothers. We had a code of honor among us, and our friendship stayed strong because of it. We were soon to find out just how strong we needed to be.

10

THE KNIFE

The weather was cool during the spring, but by midday the sun was warm and pleasant. Before breakfast and before school classes started, my friends Pioter and Edmund and I would go to the back of the outhouses, warm ourselves in the morning sun, and tell stories. We called this place Argentina.

The name came from an enchanting story our teacher read to us. It was a story about a boy who lived in the magical place of perpetual sunshine and was surrounded by an orchard full of exotic fruit trees. Boys could have adventures and their pick of the orchard's bounty. It was our version of paradise, and the name of the book was Argentina.

We blocked off our fairy-tale place by piling some stones around the area to form a kind of rough wall. We each had our personal rock to sit on. When we started learning our ABCs, we scratched our names in our rocks.

In our Argentina we had an unobstructed view of the sand dunes across the road, and the distant mountains. The dry grasslands beyond the road were quite beautiful and looked desolate except when the Uzbeks on donkeys traveled east across them toward the mountains. Sometimes a southern wind would blow over the outhouse in our direction, so we had to move, but most of the time we tolerated the odor.

After breakfast we usually had to attend school. I was placed in first grade. I was six years old. Our school curriculum consisted of the Polish alphabet, addition and subtraction, and the Soviet version of Polish history. But much of the school's curriculum centered on indoctrination. We were exposed to a good number of myths about Comrade Stalin and his exploits. Pictures of Stalin were everywhere, as were photos of Lenin and Marx. I still remember some of the patriotic songs we learned to sing glorifying Stalin and the Soviet Union.

Marx, Lenin, Stalin

Czar Nicholas II was ousted from power during the Bolshevik Revolution of 1917. Although the Czar abdicated on March 2, 1917, he and his family and attendants were executed in the summer of 1918. Vladimir Lenin led the Bolshevik Revolution against the Russian Provisional Government and rose to power. As Chairman of the Council of People's Commissars, Lenin was influenced by philosopher and social scientist Karl Marx, who advocated for socialism and a classless society—"from each according to his abilities, to each according to his needs."

Upon Lenin's death, two former colleagues vied for power: Leon Trotsky and Joseph Stalin. The

> *struggle for power was won by Joseph Stalin, the head of the Communist Party, who became the leader of the Soviet Union until his death in 1953. He sent Trotsky into exile and had him assassinated in 1940 in Mexico where Trotsky was living at the time. Stalin developed a five-year plan to bring Soviet industry into the modern age. It is estimated that he also ruthlessly killed twenty million political opponents—government officials as well as citizens.*

The instructions were all given in the Polish language, and, oddly, we were never required to learn how to read or write Russian. These indoctrination classes would generally end by noon in time for lunch.

After lunch it was playtime, and the teachers attempted to keep order on the playground. A couple of bullies were difficult to handle, but they were lone wolves with no followers. Consequently, fights were kept to a minimum on the playground.

Pioter, Edmund, and I would meet after school in sunny Argentina if the weather wasn't too hot and the wind was blowing from the right direction. There we would talk and play checkers or a pebble game. In the pebble game you throw a pebble in the air, then you quickly pick up a pebble on the ground with the same hand, and before the airborne pebble falls to the ground, you must catch it with the same hand.

Argentina was a place where we could be apart from the other kids and pretend how we would change the world if we had the power to do so. I remember once saying that if I ever had enough to eat, I would never ask for anything more, and the others agreed.

True hunger is like an urge you have in your mind and body that never goes away. When you are truly hungry, you always know you are hungry. Your stomach and brain always tell you that. You think about it all the time. Hunger is a pain you can never satisfy as long as you lack enough to eat. When you finally do get satisfied, it is a feeling you never forget.

Across the Black Road adjacent to our property flowed a stream. And across the stream was located a fenced-off orchard visible from the children's home. A long mesh fence enclosed the orchard, and the front of the fence was set several feet from the bank of the stream. The orchard was owned or operated by Uzbek farmers.

Large uruk trees hugged the inside of the fence and their branches extended over the stream. In late spring and summer the fruit on the uruk trees would ripen, and some of the uruk fruit would fall into the stream. The kids from the children's home would stand in the shallow water of the stream waiting for the uruk to fall in the stream so we could scoop up the fruit and eat it.

Often the three of us would join the other kids to fish for the uruk floating in the stream. After a while we realized that from eating the green uruk, our bellies would swell up and cause horrible diarrhea. We had to wait until the fruit was ripe, but by then the Uzbeks would harvest the uruk, and there was little fruit left to scavenge.

In the fall of 1943, I was about six and a half years old, and both Pioter and Edmund were slightly older. One day I had an encounter with a much older boy who was known to be a bully. He wanted me to give him the bread Mother left for me. I refused. Pioter and Edmund heard the commotion.

They immediately came to my aid before the bully could hit me, and together we had that kid begging for mercy.

I shared with Pioter and Edmund some of the food Mother brought me, and that further cemented our friendship. Edmond and I were Jewish, and Pioter was Catholic. We never talked about religion; besides, none of us knew much about it. In many ways Pioter was more like me than Edmund. We were more apt than Edmund to stand our ground, take chances, and not flee at the first sign of danger. Pioter and I seemed to have understood each other like only true friends could. It came to serve us well.

Pioter, Edmund, and I arranged our cots so that they were close to each other in our sleeping room where at most two dozen of us slept. There was just enough room between the cots to walk by. We were like three peas in a pod. The army-style cots had wooden frames. No springs. They lay close to the ground, yet there was just enough space underneath to store some stuff, like our shoes. There was also a cardboard box under each cot for keeping personal items or a change of clothes.

Our clothes did not consist of much. I had a warm jacket, two pair of pants—one long and one short. I had two pair of underwear. We turned them inside out to wear them on both sides before an occasional washing. I had just one pair of socks—full of holes. My only shoes were worn and beat up.

Raids and Beatings

The orchard and the collective vegetable farm a few miles down the road were magnets for starving kids. Several kids from the children's home got caught raiding the vegetable farm and the orchard. The guards from the vegetable farm would just take the kids' stash away, kick their behinds, and let them go, but the guards from the orchard would give the kids a severe beating and bring them to David, the superintendent of the children's home, during playground time so everyone could see their bloody faces.

On a few occasions the beatings were so harsh that the children had to be hospitalized. David would call the police on those beatings, but they were unresponsive. The Uzbeks were the most dangerous to tangle with. They were the biggest thieves in the orchard and did not tolerate competition. Uzbeks had an unforgiving nature. They also had vicious dogs guarding the perimeter of the fence and didn't hesitate to beat or kill anyone caught stealing.

The vegetable farm was a little less risky, but it was much more difficult to get there. During the vegetable season we would wait until evening before we went to the farm. There we would hide in the brush like wolves until the last worker left. Then we would harvest several small sacks of tomatoes, cucumbers, and carrots.

When the uruk in the orchard were ripe enough to eat and the other fruits were beginning to ripen, we were ready. We made a long stick with a hook on the end and used it to reach some of the fallen fruit lying on the ground next to the fence. Once in a while one of us would slide under the fence and put the fruit in a bag, and the other two would pull him back by his feet. That only worked when there was fruit on the ground close to the fence.

The fruits that ripened in summer, such as pears and apples, were much farther from the fence, requiring us to enter the orchard. Inside the fence we had to be alert and employ high-risk maneuvers. To avoid getting caught, we had to successfully outsmart the dogs, remember where in the fence the tunnel was located, and avoid the Uzbek workers. During that year we learned how to supplement our diet with fruits and vegetables—and not get caught.

Haia and My Mother

When Haia, an educated woman, read the papers to us out loud, we felt we had a better, truer understanding of what was really happening in the world. Up until now, the only news we heard was from others through rumor and gossip.

She was our interpreter, analyst, and commentator all rolled into one. A typical Soviet dispatch from the frontlines would say something to the effect that "our glorious soldiers" have taken such and such a city, which she told us actually meant they were still fighting. If it reported that "our glorious soldiers have captured a town, wiped out the enemy, and are moving to the next town," she said it meant they were bogged down in a bitter stalemate. If it claimed that "our glorious soldiers have defeated the enemy," she said that meant that they had most certainly lost. The reports were all about saving face.

I believe Haia was a little older than my mother, who at that time was a young woman of twenty-five. Haia had strange features. She was not a particularly attractive woman, but when she talked and smiled, her pleasant personality really came out.

Haia was the only person who made sense in that entire crazy world we were caught up in. She warned my mother not to steal too much or to keep too much for her and me, reminding Mother, "You've got to give a little bit to everybody or otherwise they'll report you." As bright as Haia was, she relied on my mother because she did not have the guts to do half the things my mother did to survive.

Because everybody craved a cigarette, tobacco became one of the most coveted items you could have for the purpose of offering bribes or doing barters. And my mother's work in the tobacco factory put her in a position of being able to get a valuable commodity to trade for favors.

She was a woman with a mission. She would not let anyone or anything stand in her way. She would get in people's faces if she felt a need to. My mother was also very generous. She freely shared everything she had under the most difficult circumstances. That willingness to share made her friends and allies.

The Bandits

As dangerous as it was, the Black Road was also difficult to avoid because it was one of the main arteries for trade and commerce in the area. Its infamous reputation was widely known. There were stories of bandits who captured and killed children and sold their flesh as meat at the bazaar. That may have been fiction.

What was real, though, was when the police caught some thieves, they hung the bandits at the bazaar. Staff from the children's home took us young boys down to the bazaar to show us how bandits die. If the intent was to burn that image in my mind and to scare me from stealing, it worked. Well, it partly worked because my friends and I continued raiding the orchard and garden.

If you traveled on that road and had any valuables or food, you took your life in your hands. People were hungry and some would do anything out of desperation. In that environment the strong preyed on the weak. This happened not only on the Black Road but in the city. When the predators saw someone in the city who was weak or ready to die, they would rob them of their clothes or shoes and just leave the person there in the street to die.

My mother wanted to visit me more often, but she couldn't because sometimes the Black Road and surrounding countryside were too dangerous to traverse. Periodically the Russians had to send in the police or the army to clear out the criminals because it was too dangerous to walk on the Black Road.

The winter of 1944 was colder than usual. Food was in short supply. Mother was ill herself, so she made fewer trips to visit me. My friends and I would go to Argentina on sunny days and plan how we would raid the orchard and the vegetable farm when the appropriate season arrived.

In spring and summer of 1944 we three had two injuries, a close call, but no deaths. Edmund got stuck under the fence when the dog was after him. In the excitement he couldn't find the tunnel under the fence until he saw us standing in front of it. Fortunately, we managed to fight off the dog with our long stick and pull Edmund through the fence. He ended up with eight stitches and a scar on his back.

One late summer evening we were hiding in the bushes as usual waiting for everyone to leave the vegetable field. An Uzbek dressed in a turban and a Russian dressed in Western clothes were the last two workers to leave. Then all of a sudden the Uzbek pulled his curved knife and cut the Russian. The Russian managed to take a switchblade from his pocket and stab the Uzbek repeatedly. The Uzbek fell to the ground dead.

The Russian looked around to see if anyone saw him, then took something from the Uzbek's pocket, and ran away. As he was running, he threw away the switchblade, and it landed in the bushes not too far from where we were hiding.

Pioter and Edmund urged me, "Mendel, we must run away from here."

I said, "You two go, but I am going to stay until I find that knife."

Edmund took off, but Pioter stayed with me until I found the knife. I was seven years old then, but I felt fully grown up. The blade was full of blood that I wiped off on some leaves. Then we made a dash toward our building in the children's home before the entrance doors were locked for the night.

The next morning we came to Argentina early so we could closely examine our new treasure. It was a beautiful, nicely balanced switchblade knife. It had a white pearl handle, and on one side two Russian initials were engraved.

When the button on the handle was pressed in one direction, the blade would be ejected from the handle with significant force, and when pressed in the other direction, the blade would retract into the handle.

We all loved that knife. It added immensely to our feeling of security. Everyone understood that this was my knife, and I carried it on me when we went on our food gathering excursions. When we were in the children's home during daytime activities and at night, I would hide the knife by burying it in a secret place behind a rock located in Argentina.

To add to their security, Pioter and Edmund fashioned for themselves heavy walking sticks from branches of the uruk tree. They used the knife to shape their walking sticks the way they wanted them to look. When we went out to scavenge for food, all three of us felt we were fully armed.

One evening we were heading back to the children's home. Some apples had spilled into the ditch from a horse-drawn wagon hauling apples to the warehouse for storage. So we scooped them up in whatever we had to carry them back.

A drunken Uzbek was riding his donkey on the Black Road, barely keeping his balance. He was loud and swearing in both Uzbek and Russian. When he saw we were carrying apples, he jumped off the donkey and came over and ripped open my shirt. My stolen apples fell to the ground. In his native tongue he barked at me, "*Carapchuk* (thief). I'll teach you thieves something."

He grabbed his knife—one of those curved Arabian knives—and lunged at my throat. I jumped back with arms outstretched. He missed my throat but cut me in my right armpit.

The Uzbek was fearsome. He had a shaved head. His eyes were sort of slanted. He had a flat nose and spoke with a deep voice. His native dress included baggy pants, shoes with tassels, and a jacket halfway opened showing his chest. He smelled horrible. I can still smell him. He was a burly, heavy-set man who looked as if he could tear me apart with his hands alone.

When he said he was going to teach us a lesson and took out his knife and came after us, we knew our lives were in danger.

Pioter quickly grabbed his walking stick by the thin side and hit the Uzbek on the head with the heavy part of the stick. The Uzbek became unsteady, went down on his knees, and dropped the knife. My adrenalin kicked in, and I quickly grabbed my knife from my pocket and stabbed him first in the throat. As the Uzbek was reaching for his knife, I stabbed him twice more in the stomach.

The look of shock in the bandit's eyes and the blood streaming from his throat wound were sights none of us ever forgot. Somehow the Uzbek managed to very slowly pick up his knife, get on his donkey, and ride away. The donkey with his human cargo on its back slowly continued down the Black Road as though it knew where it was heading. At the orchard gate the Uzbek fell off the donkey and died on the Black Road.

I took off my shirt and wiped the blood off my knife with it. I then wrapped the shirt around my armpit in an effort to stop the bleeding. Before running to the clinic, I hid the knife in our usual place.

The nurse in the clinic said, "What in the hell did you get involved in?" Before I could answer, she said, "Don't tell me. I don't want to know!"

I asked her not to tell my mother. The nurse replied, "I can't tell her anything since I know nothing."

Before we left the clinic, she said in an earnest tone, "My advice to you boys is to stay away from the orchard. These Uzbeks are mean people, and if they catch you stealing, they will cut your throat without giving it a second thought."

We expected the police to come around and interrogate some of the children. But all they wanted to know is if anyone saw a knife fight. One of the policeman said the dead man was a mean drunk and troublemaker who worked in the orchard across the road. Then the policeman added, "He just got into one knife fight too many, and this time he was found dead."

From the blood trail, they deduced that the knife fight took place on the Black Road in front of the children's home.

My wound required about ten stitches, and I was bedridden with a high fever for about a week. I also had terrible nightmares about the killing and so did my friends. I told mother I injured myself climbing a tree and never said anything more about it to her or anyone else. Mother came and brought me some medication for the infection, and I am sure that helped a great deal.

Pioter and I quickly put the knifing behind us, but Edmund had a harder time with it. We all realized that we acted in self-defense and could have just as easily ended up dead. So we agreed not say anything to anyone about the incident, nor should we talk about it anymore. That was the end of the story, except, of course, when we sat in our Argentina and played our games, we talked about it all the time.

On November 6, 1943, the Russian forces took Kiev, and from then on the Soviet forces were unstoppable. Then on June 6, 1944, D-Day, the Western Allies invaded Normandy, a beach in northern France and gateway to retaking Europe, sealing Germany's fate in the war.

On July 8, 1944, the Soviet deputy foreign minister, Andrei Vishinski, informed the Polish ambassador that the entire Anders Army had permission to leave the Soviet Union. In addition, up to 70,000 Polish civilians could be evacuated with them. About 15,000 children from the orphanages were in the first wave to leave for Tehran, Iran. Of those, 1,000 Jewish orphans were collected from the various Polish childrens' homes and evacuated. The Jewish children were handed over to the Jewish agency in Tehran, and despite many obstacles, the Jewish agency managed to smuggle them into Palestine.

A Shot in the Dark

Pioter's uncle fought with a Polish unit at the battle of Kiev and was killed; however, his family didn't get a letter acknowledging his death until March 1944. Pioter didn't know much about his uncle but was concerned about his father, who was in the same unit.

Of course I had no idea what happened to my father, so Pioter tried to make me feel good by speculating that maybe both of our fathers were in the Polish Army fighting side by side against the Nazis. Then Pioter started laughing out loud, "Won't they be surprised to learn how we spent the war together in this place!"

It was a game we played when we listened to the radio as the Red Army was taking town by town. We pretended our fathers were involved in every battle and would come back as heroes.

I was interviewed to be taken to Iran with other Jewish orphans, but was rejected because I was not a full orphan. Besides, Mother would not consider it, and I didn't want to go. However, some of the children from our children's home were evacuated.

During the 1944 growing season, the Uzbeks in the orchard eased up a little. Apparently a new management team took over because the old team got caught stealing. To our surprise the new foreman from the orchard came over to talk to David. He told David they were not heartless people and they understood that the children were driven to steal by hunger, "But the fruit we grow is earmarked for the war effort, so we can't permit anyone, including our employees, to take what they want unhindered."

Although he agreed not to beat children caught stealing, he said they would hand them over to the police, who were no angels either. He did allow, though, for children to continue fishing in the stream for uruk and to pick up the fruit next to the fence.

He went on, "For your protection you must do it in the stream in front of the children's home where you can be seen because there are a lot of bandits roaming the Black Road."

David called us into his office where we found a room full of kids who had been known to raid the orchard. David started by telling us about the bandits and the kidnapping rings operating on the Black Road. Then he laid down new rules about behavior on the playground and the orchard. He told us that since the property had no fence, that even on the playgrounds we should stay in groups and not cross the Black Road alone. David further made it very clear that any child caught inside the orchard would be automatically expelled and assigned to a different children's home.

We played by the rules throughout the summer of 1944. Mother was doing well in her tobacco business, which meant she came more often to see me with her buttermilk and other food. Mother had put on some weight and purchased for herself a new *fufaika* (a sheepskin leather coat of rough brown hide with fur cuffs and collar). She wore that *fufaika* in winter and summer. It was a status symbol among her friends.

By fall of that year the war was going well for the Red Army, and Mother felt that by next year we would be back home in Pabianice. So she began buying things for herself and the return trip home. In school they started teaching us the Polish anthem, patriotic songs, and heroic stories of the Polish past.

Our group still met in Argentina, and the question of food always came up. We stayed away from the orchard, but from time to time the foreman would bring David a couple of bags of overripe fruit as a gesture of good faith. In many ways it was a lazy summer. Our teacher took us on excursions to the Islamic mosques that lay in ruin. She attempted to tell us how old the city of Samarkand was and how many times the city had been conquered by invading armies.

Fruit and vegetables from several outlying collective farms were stored in a warehouse next to the rice factory located upstream next to the Black Road. In one of our Argentina meetings Pioter and I suggested that we check out the place and see if we could get our hands on some fruit. Edmund didn't want to participate.

He said, "The guards there have guns, and they may shoot us. Besides we shouldn't be going on the Black Road while the bandits are free to roam there." We knew Edmund was right, but Pioter and I just wanted to check things out, so we went alone.

The warehouse had a loading dock where horse-drawn wagons were lined up next to the dock ready to be unloaded. The warehouse was fenced in, but one wagon was right next to the fence. So we reached in and each of us grabbed a couple of peaches. As we were running away down the road, two shots rang out. We figured the shots were meant to scare us. It worked, so we just kept on running until we reached the entrance to the children's home.

When we stopped, I said to Pioter, "My shoes are wet, when did we step in water?" He looked down and told me that I was bleeding. I didn't feel the pain of being shot and didn't even drop the peaches.

The pain began when I saw the blood and looked at my knee. It hurt even more when the nurse in the clinic cleaned the wound with iodine and began stitching me up. I was shot in the right knee, but I was lucky that the bullet missed the bone. The nurse didn't ask any questions. She bandaged me up and told me to stay off the playground for a week.

Before we left the clinic, the nurse warned us to stay off the Black Road. "These bandits on the road are soldiers returning from the war. They don't want to register for work, so they engage in criminal activities, and they all have guns." She implied that I was shot by one of the returning soldiers. So Pioter and I agreed with her, even though that's not exactly what happened.

In August during the mosquito season, the children's home had an outbreak of malaria. Many children were infected, but not all came down with the sickness. I suspect I was one of those who was infected, but the brunt of the illness didn't manifest itself until a year later as the chills and fever can often be delayed. The use of DDT was just beginning to be used to keep the mosquito population down.

Then in September the home had a lice epidemic, and many of the children and some adults came down with typhoid fever. Edmund was also sick with a fever for about a week. Pioter and I had already had typhoid, so were not affected.

In order to keep the epidemic from spreading to the rest of the community, health officials came in and moved us all outdoors. They boiled all the bedding and clothing. For two days just about everyone walked around in his underwear, except for the girls. Then they fumigated all the buildings, and when we got our clothes back, we were doused with DDT powder.

Being free of lice, even for a short time, was an incredible relief. To get rid of that constant itch was certainly worth the inconvenience of the delousing procedure. The epidemic was horrible. Both the children and teachers who were infected had to be isolated. They suffered greatly, and many of them died.

On January 14, 1945, the Russian forces reached East Prussia. Some of the Nazi labor and concentration camps were liberated by the Red Army. We knew because Edmund was notified that his mother, who somehow ended up in a Nazi labor camp, was alive, and they would be reunited as soon as the hostilities ended. He was just ecstatic, running around showing everyone the letter, which was written in Yiddish. None of us could read Yiddish, but David could, so he translated the letter for Edmund.

Edmund kept his mother's letter with him all the time. He no longer wanted to take any chances and go on food raids with us. Edmund's attitude about everything changed. He now had something to live for. His mother would depend on him since he was the only man in the family left alive.

11

DANGER ON THE BLACK ROAD

Pioter and I continued fishing for uruk in the stream and collecting the fruit next to the fence with our stick. There was no need to make raids inside the orchard because the orchard workers became friendlier to us and often would deliberately leave some fruit next to the fence.

In the spring of 1945, the Black Road became even more dangerous to travel. Mother had to hire armed policemen to go with her when she came to see me. Besides robberies, there were kidnappings and stabbings. A young girl from the children's home was beaten and raped and returned only after a ransom was paid. An older boy was killed and left on the road not far from the children's home. All of us children were given instructions again to stay together in groups and not to stray far from the grounds.

The police captured about ten of the bandits and hung them in the middle of the bazaar for all to see. The authorities claimed these bandits were Tatars, but to us they looked like regular Uzbeks and Russians. These events created a climate of fear, and ridiculous rumors were flying about.

At night I slept with the knife beside me, and during the day I kept it in my pocket or somewhere close where I could get to it quickly. The three of us were on edge and couldn't decide whether going out to scavenge for food was worth the risk. So we sat in our Argentina and debated the risk/reward options regarding our predicament.

One evening the three of us sat in Argentina watching the sun go down. I went to the outhouse, and Pioter and Edmund were in the back. Then I heard Pioter scream, "Mendel! Mendel! Dig up your knife! Edmund was kidnapped!"

As I came out, we saw a wiry young man in a dirty Russian uniform holding Edmund with a brown sack over his head. The bandit looked like a skeleton of skin and bones. His hair was to his shoulders. His pants looked as if they wrapped around him twice. The lower buttons of his shirt were gone. His sleeves were dirty, perhaps from using them as a handkerchief. He hadn't shaved in days. His face was long and thin, his eyes red.

When he screamed at us to leave him alone, his face contorted into a grotesque mask. I remember a scar on his right cheek.

He was dragging Edmund as they were heading toward the mountains. I quickly dug up my knife from the hiding place in Argentina. By now, Pioter had a bloody nose from wrestling with the bandit. He grabbed his walking stick and said, "Mendel, you see that sand dune ahead? It is where the road to the mountains crosses the Black Road and the two roads meet. The bandit will have to take one of those roads.

If we run fast on the Black Road, we can get to the sand dune before the bandit dragging Edmond does."

We ran as hard as we could and got to the sand dune ahead of the kidnapper. Neither of us gave any thought to what we would do when confronted with the bandit dragging our friend Edmund. As the bandit got closer, our hearts were pumping. We heard Edmund crying and the bandit hitting him to stop.

As the bandit came in view, Pioter swung his walking stick as hard as he could. It surprised the bandit. As he looked our way, the stick hit him in the nose and right eye. The bandit screamed in pain. Pioter hit him again, and this time the blow landed on his head and neck. I came over and stabbed the bandit several times in his right arm and right leg so he would let Edmund go.

Our attack had caught the bandit by complete surprise, and it all happened so fast that the bandit had no time to react. He had no idea who we were or how many of us there were. Somehow the bandit picked himself up and started hobbling away in great pain.

We grabbed Edmund and made our way back to the children's home as fast as we could. As we were turning from the Black Road to the children's home, we stopped to look, and from that distance we could see the kidnapper still hobbling until he disappeared from view under the twilight sky.

When we finally caught our breath, we were all shaking with excitement. Pioter had a broken nose from a direct punch he received. Edmund was all shaken up and had a few bruises on his face and back. I was uninjured except for fingernail scratches from the bandit as he was trying to grab my arm when I was stabbing him. We jumped up and down laughing and screaming, "We are heroes! We are heroes!"

That Night None of Us Could Sleep

The next day we told David that a bandit dressed in a dirty Russian Army uniform attempted to kidnap Edmund and that we managed to free him. We didn't elaborate on the facts because the knife connected us to the death of the Uzbek. Later in Argentina we asked ourselves, "Have we killed the bandit?"

"I hope so," said Edmund. Pioter and I were not sure, but one thing we were sure of, the bandit left in a great deal of hurt.

We also wondered where we got the courage to do this. At first, without much thought we simply responded to an emergency and, in the excitement, decided to pursue the bandit. We finally realized that we could have been killed. In retrospect, the scariest part was the prospect of being captured and sold into slavery. We succeeded because we acted without thinking or considering the consequences and let the adrenaline take over.

Shortly after the incident, the police made several raids on the bandits' mountain hideouts and arrested most of them who were committing the crimes on the Black Road. For the rest of the year, we stayed close to the compound, except for the time a wagon full of fruit turned over in a ditch because of a broken wheel. Before the driver could get help, the kids swarmed the spilled fruit on the ground and carried most of it away, and we were among them.

During the day, our salvation was Argentina, just the three of us in our secret "clubhouse" without walls.

Of course we talked about all kinds of things. We talked about politics to some extent, about how far the Soviet army would get in its push into Germany and when they would liberate Poland. We knew anti-Semitism existed, but

I thought it was a part of nature—that that was just how people were. We knew that people killed each other. At ages seven and eight, we didn't try to analyze why. We were just thinking how to survive the situation, how to outlast the war. The war was always on our minds.

We rehashed the movies we saw on the flickering projector flashing black-and-white images on a sheet tacked to the wall in the dining hall. The cord was snaked into the kitchen where the only electricity was located. We children would sit at the dining tables and be taken to faraway places and situations with cowboy star Tom Mix or through the clowning around of Charlie Chaplin. We identified with the cohorts in one of the early Hollywood versions of *The Three Musketeers*.

We talked about what we were going to do when we got back home. We talked about what good friends we were going to be for the rest of our lives. We made a pact that whoever had enough food would have to invite the others to feast on it. Pioter, Edmund, and I, like everybody else, constantly had food on our minds. Hunger set the daily agenda.

We honestly thought Argentina (the country) was America. We did not know the distinction between the two. A few years later, when my family crossed the Atlantic en route to the United States, I declared, "Well, we're finally going to see Argentina." I still didn't realize it was a completely different country.

The End of WWII

The surrender of the German Army to the Western Allies (U.S., Britain, and France) and to the Soviet Union took place in several stages during the months of April and May 1945. Adolf Hitler committed suicide on April 30, 1945.

Some units of the German Army continued to fight, but all German armed forces surrendered unconditionally after an instrument of surrender was signed May 7, 1945, at Reims, France. The surrender took effect and was publicly announced the following day, May 8, and is celebrated as VE Day (Victory in Europe Day) in the United States.

The surrender took effect at 11 p.m. Central European Time. In more eastern time zones, this was already the following day. That is why Russia and other countries in Eastern Europe celebrate May 9 as Victory Day.

Millions of people took to the streets in celebration, in London, New York, Moscow, and other cities around the world.

12

I OUTLASTED THE WAR

Once we heard the war in Europe had ended, we had a special going-home party where we were given Polish jackets and all the food we could eat. This was the first time during the entire war that I walked away from the table satisfied.

We continued to meet in our Argentina and were very much excited about the prospect of going home to Poland. David made an announcement that the children from the Polish children's home would be going back to Poland as a group, so we were on standby and needed to be ready when the transport was made available to us. We were happy because that meant we would be traveling together and might have a chance to meet each other's parents in Poland.

Mother came to visit me more often and sometimes would even bring her friend Haia and another woman friend from Pabianice. Mother and her friends didn't know how or when they would be able to leave.

World War II was over for most people in the world. We didn't know it at the time, but the war wasn't over for the Jews.

Shortly after the end of all hostilities, the Russian authorities announced they had dropped all charges against us Polish citizens deported to Russia. They also informed all Poles in Samarkand that they would be repatriated and permitted to return to their home of origin. At first, only those with Polish passports were permitted to return, but later all Poles were permitted to go home.

In the spring of 1946, Mother had a choice either to take me with her on the transport or pick me up at the children's home in Breslau, Poland. All children and staff were to be transported together from Samarkand to Breslau first, ahead of the parents and other adults. The rest of the transports would start two weeks later. If she decided to send me with the other children on the train, she would be assigned to the first adult train leaving Samarkand to Breslau about a week later.

Mother was told the children would receive special rations, medical treatment, and new clothing on their journey. In Poland the children would be housed in a nice facility with children their own age until she picked me up. Mother's memory of the crowded and unsanitary journey to Samarkand guided her judgment, so she reluctantly let me travel with the other kids back to Poland. Besides, Mother gave her usual bribes to several key staffers to keep an eye on me and make sure they didn't let me get into trouble.

Finally, we were instructed that trucks were coming to get us the next day. We had a good meal the night before. There was bread, potatoes, buttermilk, and salami. That was a big deal and as close to a feast as we ever had there. We didn't sleep that night; the anticipation was too great.

A group portrait of Polish-Jewish refugee children in a children's home outside Uzbekistan shortly before they were repatriated to Poland. This is not the same group the author lived with. This photo is from the United States Holocaust Memorial Museum, courtesy of Irene Rogers.

The morning of our departure, Pioter, Edmund, and I went out to Argentina. We got to talking very excitedly about finally being able to go home. We reminisced about what Poland looked like. We talked about smells and food and how nice it was going to be to have enough to eat when we got home. We had been just small children when the Nazis rousted us from our homes. Now we were older boys, about nine years old, who had seen far too many atrocities and done acts way beyond our years. We were different.

We became so wrapped up in conversation that we lost track of the time. The trucks were almost getting ready to leave before we realized we had better join the others. In our rush to catch up, I forgot the knife.

I had kept it in its hiding place until the last possible moment because the staff were checking us for contraband that morning, and I didn't want them to find it on me. But in our haste the knife escaped my mind. I regretted leaving that knife behind because it had meant so much to us. The impact it had on me was such that I retained a fascination with knives that continues to this day. I have always collected knives and carried one on me. It is partly for nostalgia and partly for protection, and I suppose it's something that keeps me connected to that time when a knife was the difference between life and death.

I didn't have much to pack. I wore most of my clothing. The three of us made sure we stood next to each other so we could be loaded on the truck transport to the train station together. It was a bumpy ride to the station, and on the way we used profane words when we passed a place we didn't like or had a problem with.

At the station Mother and her two friends waited for us to arrive so they could say goodbye to me. They all hugged me, and Mother kissed me very hard. She handed me a bag of food and said, "I am leaving a week from today on the train, and when I get to Poland, we will look for your father if he is still alive."

When the train began moving, I stood on the top bunk, looked out the window, and saw my mother on the train platform crying. It just broke my heart. I wanted to jump off the train and go to her. I felt guilty leaving Mother all alone shedding tears and looking so sad.

We settled in our boxcar and adjusted to life on the train. The boxcars were empty but clean. Each contained four sections of double wooden bunk beds. A wide aisle ran the width of the boxcar, and a narrower aisle ran the length of the car. At each end of the narrow aisle was a sit-down toilet and basin to wash up. There was even a privacy curtain surrounding the latrine. Each of the four corners of the boxcar had two small square windows. In the middle were stacked four rows of mattresses.

We had assigned bunks, and each one of us was instructed to grab a mattress and put it on our assigned bunk. The blankets, pillows, and the aluminum eating utensils (a spoon, a knife, and a canteen cup for drinking) were issued to us later. Pioter and I had a double bunk beneath a window. He slept on the bottom bunk, and I slept on top. Edmund was given a bunk across the aisle, and we could signal to each other.

There were only twenty to twenty-five children to a boxcar and two teachers to keep the peace. Compared to the accommodations we had coming to Samarkand, the ones leaving were much superior. I couldn't help but wonder what my mother's train travel would be like. I was hoping that she, too, would have a pleasant trip back, and when we met, we could talk about the future and leave the past behind us.

Fears Followed Us

During the daytime the sliding doors were kept partially open so we could get some fresh air. But at nights or when it was cool, the door and window shutters were closed.

Our first stop was Tashkent. There we joined the Trans-Caspian Railway that follows the path of the ancient Silk Road through much of western Central Asia. The western track took us across Kazakhstan with stops at Aktau Port on the Caspian Sea, Ganyushkino near the Russian border, and from there all the way to Moscow. This was a much shorter route than traveling by the Trans-Siberian line, and the weather was much warmer as well.

Most of the journey back was pleasant, and we didn't have to compete with the Red Army for the tracks. We had several scheduled stops where we actually got off the train and went sightseeing. Of all the stops, Moscow was the most memorable. The teacher took us for a city tour. It was obvious that the city had experienced heavy bombardment. The destruction was massive, with debris everywhere, but the underground subway was unaffected. People were working at clearing the rubble off the streets, and for the most part, the main streets were passable.

We were in Moscow for about four or five days, and everywhere we went people treated us as if we were the children of dignitaries.

Our teacher also took us on the underground, and after a short ride we came up to a building near the Kremlin. In this impressive building, we had lunch with a Russian general and other officials. One of the boys asked if he could see the general's medals. The general found the request amusing, but as the other children started saying, "Me too, me too," the general consented. We all surrounded the general. Then he began pointing to each of his medals and patiently explained which battle each medal represented.

We sang some patriotic songs in Russian for the Soviet dignitaries at the request of the teacher escorting us. The teacher wanted to show us off. I can still remember the lyrics to the songs today: "If tomorrow is the war, then we're going to get ready for war."

I think the Soviets were trying to brainwash us because they saw us as the next generation of Poles, and since we had been liberated from captivity, they expected us to be grateful, loyal subjects of the Mother Land. Everything in the Soviet Union had an ulterior motive behind it. Which is why, before we departed, the general told us to be sure to tell our parents that the brave Red Army freed Poland and saved us all from the Nazi butchers.

At the time we weren't quite sure what to make of that statement, but shortly afterward we were shocked to learn precisely what he meant. Back on the train the teacher attempted to prepare us for what evil people the German soldiers were, so she told us a mild version of the concentration camps. We had no idea what she was talking about. It was too unbelievable to be true, so we didn't believe her.

It took us slightly over a month to get from Samarkand to Bialystok, almost two months less than our previous trip from Arkhangelsk to Samarkand. Of course the journey back was much different than the one going. In Bialystok we changed trains and from there went by normal passenger train, not cattle cars or boxcars with wooden bunks.

The passenger train gave me my first glimpse at a flush toilet. When I went into the bathroom, I looked at this white porcelain contraption and didn't know what to make of it. I peered into the toilet bowl and saw water, but I was afraid to go in it because I thought the water was for cleaning up after.

I must have been sitting in that bathroom for about forty-five minutes wondering what to do, when I finally screwed up the courage to ask the escort where to do my business.

She came inside and explained, "Well, you sit down here and go and then you pull this chain and it will clean up after you."

It was a new experience. That was also the first time I used toilet paper. Before that it was always copies of *Pravda* or some other newspaper.

We traveled in comfort southwest across Poland to the city of Breslau (now Wroclaw) and an uncertain future.

At the start of the war my mother and father, brother Hershel and I (and later my baby brother Velvel) were a cohesive family. We stayed together through all our struggles and tribulations in Russia until my father left the train near Novosibirsk. Now Mother was on a train a week behind me. Hershel and Velvel were dead, and then there was Father, but no one knew what happened to him.

These thoughts ran through my mind, and the question on what would happen next became my nightmare. Often, in the middle of the night, I would wake up screaming, not knowing where I was. I was not the only one, so the teachers were used to it and only in severe cases would they intervene. We boys had lived with a lot of anxieties. Our parents were someplace else. It was difficult not to think the worst. Those fears followed us.

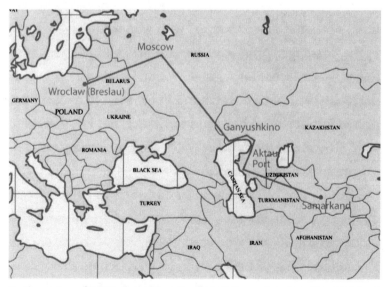

In the spring of 1946, the author finally left Samarkand and headed back to Breslau, Poland, by train.

The Nazi Killing Machine

Beginning in 1933 the Nazis began to detain political prisoners, and later Jews, the physically and mentally handicapped, homosexuals, Roma (Gypsies), Jehovah's Witnesses, and anyone who opposed them, in concentration camps. Prisoners in these camps had their heads shaved, were stripped of possessions, were given subsistence diets, and inadequate clothing. Prisoners of Auschwitz lost their identity when they were tattooed with numbers on their forearms.

Researchers at the United States Holocaust Memorial Museum documented in 2013 some 42,500 Nazi ghettos and camps that were used for three primary functions: transit, forced labor, and extermination. A transit camp was a holding camp for prisoners until they could be shipped to other camps.

Forced labor camps worked prisoners long hours, starved them with a diet of as little as 300 calories per day, provided minimal clothing and demanded work for which they were ill-equipped. The prisoners worked with arms and ammunition, mining, railroad and tunnel construction, farming, and sometimes pointless excessive labor. The Nazis called this forced labor "extermination through work" and estimated that few prisoners survived more than thirty days in a labor camp. The labor camps were primarily in the West and Poland.

Extermination camps in the East were six in number, although death came in all the camps due to starvation and illness. Prisoners were methodically executed at camps called Chelmo, Belzec, Sobibor, Treblinka, Majdanek, and Auschwitz-Birkenau. A prisoner who was not able to work was likely killed hours after arrival at a camp. Prisoners were shot or gassed and their bodies buried in mass graves or incinerated in huge furnaces.

When the U.S., British, and Soviet forces discovered these camps, they began to learn the full extent of the Nazi atrocities. They encountered skeletal corpses and hollow-eyed prisoners who were merely skin and bone. Many of the prisoners died after well-intentioned Allied soldiers fed them food that their starved bodies could not digest.

It is estimated that the Nazis killed fifteen to twenty million people during the Holocaust. Two thirds of the Jewish population of Europe was eradicated. The concentration camps claimed six million Jews. A life of starvation and disease in the ghettos, mass killings in villages and other locations, and death marches claimed the lives of others.

13

UNEXPECTED REUNIONS

We arrived in Breslau, Poland, early in the morning on a warm day in 1946. After a snack of bread and cheese, we were loaded onto buses and driven through the streets of the city. From what we could see, Breslau was not badly damaged by the war, at least not as badly as Moscow.

At one point the bus stopped for a few minutes, and out of the corner of my eye I could see a destroyed and burned synagogue. All of a sudden a big fear came over me, and I hallucinated that Abraham, the old man from the burned-out *shul*, was sitting next to me saying, "Mendel, don't be afraid, everything will be all right."

The Breslau children's home was a three-story building, and except for some bullet holes on the side of the building, it seemed to be intact—certainly an upgrade from the last one. The rooms were nice and spacious and clean. For once we had real beds to sleep in with fresh sheets and pillowcases.

When we first arrived, the staff deloused us and we took a shower. They threw away all our clothes and gave us new clothes. What a relief because we had been living with lice all over us and our clothes. Their biting was a constant irritant. You would itch and ache. Getting clear of that was like being liberated from a swarm of ants.

After a good night's sleep we had a hearty breakfast. We gorged ourselves on every morsel of food on the table—white bread for the first time—and when no one was looking, we stuffed our pockets with salami, cheese, apples, and *kuchen* (crusty fruit pie). It was my first time tasting a chocolate bar. We never knew when we'd get another meal.

It was not until we arrived in Breslau that I realized the Three Musketeers were going to suffer a separation.

Pioter and I were called in to meet with a caseworker whose job it was to unite children with their parents. She asked us both identifying questions in Polish and said she had good news. She first turned to Pioter and told him his father was alive but was now in a Lodz hospital recovering from his war wounds.

She went on to tell him, with a big smile on her face, "You should be very proud of your father. He is a war hero. After you have a chance to rest up a couple days, one of our caseworkers will take you by train to see him, and you will be reunited with him."

Pioter just sat there stunned, not knowing what to say or do. Pioter didn't really know his father. He wanted to know what happened to his mother after she dropped him off at the Samarkand children's home. The caseworker said she did not know anything about his mother. She looked through some the files and said, "No, I have nothing on her. Your father is an important officer in the army and may know what happened to your mother."

Then she turned to me and said, "Your mother is expected to arrive in a week." I was happy and anxious to see Mother again.

Then the caseworker turned to me and asked if my father's name was Chaskiel Dawidowicz.

I said, "Yes!"

"Well, he, too, is alive and will be here tomorrow to pick you up."

"Where does he live?" I asked her.

"Not too far from here," she told me. I was far more concerned about when my mother would arrive. I didn't want to go with my father.

"You are lucky," said Pioter. "Both your mother and father are alive."

"You, too, will be lucky," I told Pioter. "My good luck in Samarkand was also your good luck. There is no reason things will change now. I am sure your mother is also alive."

Pioter was picked up the next day, and that was the last time I saw him. When Pioter left, he yelled out, "Don't worry, Mendel, I will find you after I see my father!" But we both knew that was not going to happen. Pioter was leaving, and Edmund was united with his mother. They were hugging in the hallway.

All of sudden I realized I was all alone and had no one I could depend on. The first thing I noticed was that the pre-war anti-Semitism was alive and thriving in this new Poland. I was back to experiencing the name-calling, shoving, and fist fights. Inside the facility the teacher kept order, but outside the story was different. A Jewish boy was beaten up on the playground by two Poles, and they took his cap and coat. An older Jewish boy approached me and asked if I wanted to join a self-defense group of Jewish boys.

Without asking any questions, I said, "Yes!"

He told me they had brass knuckles, and when they went anywhere, they went in a group. I thought that was a good idea. Now I knew I had to get a knife. I spent over a week in this children's home and didn't like it because my friends had left. The tension and anxiety for Jewish children in the home was high. You had to pretend not to show fear or the Polish boys would just torment you all the time. That also meant that you had to be ready to fight back.

My Father Reappears

It was a beautiful, sunny day when Chaskiel came to get me. I came to think of him by his name, Chaskiel, not as my father. I wanted nothing to do with him. He had abandoned us.

People were walking the streets with their sleeves rolled up, and across the street boys were playing soccer. I was standing outside. Chaskiel rushed by me into the building, and we didn't even recognize each other.

When the caseworker introduced me to Chaskiel, he grabbed me and we hugged. He had tears in his eyes and several times repeated how sorry he was. I didn't know what he was sorry about, so I told him I was sorry too. He wanted me to come home with him right away, but I didn't want to go with him until Mother arrived. I was afraid Mother would not be able to find us.

The caseworker assured me she knew Chaskiel's address and she lived not far from him. She further assured me that she would personally bring Mother over when she arrived to get me. I don't know why, but that caseworker was so considerate to me that I completely trusted her to do what she said she would.

I agreed to go home with Chaskiel, and on the way he asked me a lot of questions about Mother and what happened to Velvel and Hershel. All of a sudden we stopped for a moment, and Chaskiel pointed across the street to an ice cream stand.

With a big smile on his face Chaskiel asked me, "How would you like an ice cream cone?"

Crossing the street to get the ice cream, he reminded me how Hershel and I loved to go with him on his deliveries because he would buy us ice cream. He then asked if there was anything else special he could buy me. I told him I would like to have a nice folding knife. He asked why, and I told him it was for self-protection and what happened to a Jewish kid on the playground. He said it was difficult to get such a knife, but he would find one.

Again Chaskiel grabbed me and lifted me off my feet to hug me. In the process I smelled his breath, and it rekindled my memory of him from before he left the train. He must have had a drink before coming to pick me up. Chaskiel looked at me as if he couldn't believe I was alive.

Then with big smile he said, "Mendel, I suppose now you are too big for me to carry you on my shoulders." He lifted me and said, "No, not yet," and he put me down. We walked the rest of the way, just talking and joking.

Chaskiel was uncharacteristically nice to me. It made me suspicious. He was like a changed man on the outside, but I had grave reservations and serious doubts as to whether he really had changed on the inside.

When we arrived at his house Chaskiel said to the woman there, "This is my son Mendel whom I told you about." She ran away crying.

So I asked, "Did I do something wrong?"

Chaskiel turned to me and said, "No. Her name is Zlata. She will be just fine once she gets to know you."

I saw two girls outside. The three-year-old, whom I later came to know as Miriam, was pushing the baby, Shoshana Rosa, in a buggy. Right then I knew something was wrong, but I didn't quite know exactly what. I didn't ask too many questions because I really did not want to know the answers.

During the entire time I stayed with Zlata, Miriam followed me around everywhere I went. It was as though Miriam knew that I was her older brother before I did.

Zlata had a hard time looking at me. I don't think she said more than two dozen words to me, except, "It's time to eat," the whole time I was there. She was kind and never raised her voice to me. I felt we liked each other, except we didn't know what to say to one another.

I felt comfortable with just Zlata in the house, but the agitation would start when Chaskiel came home. He was a difficult man to be around. When Chaskiel was there, the level of tension rose, and even when he was being kind, it generally came with a price. Then there were those smelly pigeons again. By then I was self-sufficient and knew I didn't want to be part of Chaskiel's family again.

I think it was on a Friday when the caseworker showed up with Mother, unannounced, at Chaskiel's door. I was outside playing with Miriam and the baby when I heard a recognizable voice yelling, "Mendel! Mendel!" I turned around, and there she was, wearing her *fufaika* and crying and laughing as we hugged.

True to her word, the caseworker had brought Mother, with all her luggage in hand, directly from the children's home to Chaskiel's house. The caseworker figured that Mother was meeting her husband and son, and therefore she already had a place to stay. When Chaskiel saw Mother, he didn't know what to say or do. Should he run to Mother, or should he stay and comfort Zlata?

Chaskiel looked upset. He had planned to meet Mother at the children's home, not at his door. He wanted to control the situation and avoid the scene that was about to unfold.

Mother immediately sensed there was something wrong. She looked at Chaskiel with a half-smile, like she was about to scold him. "Chaskiel, what troubles are you in now?" she asked.

When Mother walked in the house she carefully looked around. She saw Zlata with a surprised look on her face but said nothing to her. Then Mother carefully looked at Miriam and the baby and asked Chaskiel a direct question. "Are those children yours?"

He didn't answer, but Zlata answered for him. "Yes, and I am his wife. I did not know about you and your son until Chaskiel brought Mendel home with him."

Without responding to Zlata, Mother walked up to Chaskiel, spit in his face, and said, "You are responsible for the death of my babies." Chaskiel was standing there frozen, not even wiping the spit off his face.

Hellos and Goodbyes—Forever

Mother believed with all her heart that Chaskiel had left her on the train for another woman and deliberately took those ration cards with him. No other possibility existed in her mind except that he abandoned her and his own children and left them to die on that train.

Mother was so angry that she looked as if she was ready to faint. The caseworker grabbed Mother and walked her outside to get some fresh air. I finally grasped what the relationship between Chaskiel and Zlata was and what just happened. It hadn't even entered my mind that Zlata and Chaskiel were married and that the children were my half-sisters. I was not upset. It meant that Chaskiel was no longer my father, and my mother no longer had a husband.

At that moment the issues were simple to me. Chaskiel had a new family, and now Mother and I were free to go and do as we pleased.

Mother was going to take me with her when she left, but the caseworker intervened. She was a practical woman and had witnessed many similar situations. So she asked Zlata if she could keep me for a few days until Mother found a place to stay. Zlata was fine with it for the time being.

"Right now," the caseworker told Mother, "you need to get your bearings and speak with the Rabbi." She also said, "I think your son will be better off with Zlata for the next few days than at the children's home."

I suspect it would have been difficult for the caseworker to readmit me in the children's home since I was already signed out to my parents. I agreed with the caseworker because I just didn't want to go back to the children's home and knew my stay with Chaskiel was going to be brief.

For the next few days Chaskiel tried his best to treat me well, and he even bought me a nice folding knife. The knife had a mahogany handle and four-inch blade that folded into the handle. He told me to keep the knife in my suitcase because Zlata wouldn't approve. I could take it with me when we went to the park or when we just walked on the street together. I somehow felt safer with the knife, and at that time many Poles carried knives.

Poland still had a Chief Rabbi, and each Jewish community had its own Rabbi. The Rabbi had the authority in all Jewish matters such as marriage, divorce, burial, and Jewish education. These laws were still valid from the pre-war times. Later, the Communist Polish government revoked much of the Rabbis' authority in the Jewish community. Of course, by then there weren't enough Jews left to make a difference.

After Mother found an apartment, Chaskiel came over, and they had a short confrontation about getting a *get* (divorce). Chaskiel became disagreeable and refused to give her a *get*. Mother asked, "If no *get*, then what?"

He replied, "Don't worry! I am still married to you, so I will divorce my current wife and we can start where we left off."

Mother knew the kind of *dreyer* (manipulator) he could be and that he planned to drag this out as long as he could. So she took the caseworker's recommendation and went to see the Breslau Rabbi.

In 1938, when Breslau was still a German city, the Nazis had destroyed all the synagogues except one. Mother met the Rabbi in that synagogue and explained to him her predicament. The Rabbi said he would investigate the matter and asked her to gather all documentation she had and to bring any witnesses who would verify her claim. During the investigation Mother and her friend Haia were regular visitors to the synagogue, especially to the back benches that faced the enclosed billboard.

Posted on the billboard were hundreds of notes from people looking for relatives who may have survived the war. It was also a good place to get firsthand information from other survivors on what happened to people in the towns and villages they came from. Information was passed by word of mouth from people who had returned to their native villages and towns to tell what they saw.

While sitting on a bench by the billboard, Mother, Haia, and their mutual friend from Samarkand, who was also from Pabianice, were talking. Mother told them that, after she obtained a *get*, she planned to return to Pabianice to reclaim her property.

The other Pabianice woman told Mother, "Don't go back. There is nothing there for you, or any of us. I couldn't find one recognizable Jewish face in the entire city. I didn't hear a word of Yiddish spoken anywhere. The chatter from the peddlers, the sounds, smells, and the Yiddish signs are all gone. It's like waking up from a terrible nightmare and realizing you weren't asleep."

The woman's Polish neighbor from before the war told her that the Germans confiscated all the Jewish property, put all the Jews in the ghetto, and in 1942, deported them all to Lodz. That was all she knew except that one Jew who came back to claim his apartment ended up in the hospital.

In good weather there were always new faces coming by and chatting. It was also the place to find out where people were going when they decided to leave Poland for good. Several Jewish organizations informed citizens how to best get to the displaced persons (DP) camps in Western Europe, Palestine, and other countries.

One gloomy day, Mother was sitting on the bench in front of the synagogue holding some papers the Rabbi gave her and looking hopeless. Mother didn't know what to do or how to proceed. The Rabbi told Mother what those papers said, but she couldn't read them. Next to her a man sat down and started talking to her. Mother told him her predicament, and he agreed to help her fill out some of the papers she had in her hand.

After that they kept on meeting on that bench and exchanged horror stories about their lives in Russia. After a while this man and Mother hit it off, and the two of them devised a plan on their future together and on how they would deal with Chaskiel.

Displaced Persons (DP) Camps

When WWII ended, many millions of people found themselves far from home. The Allied military and civilian authorities took responsibility for these refugees and tended to their immediate needs (shelter, food, and medical care). The first goal was to send as many of the refugees back to their home countries as possible. By the end of 1945, more than six million WWII refugees had been repatriated to their countries of origin.

For others, this was not possible due to changing borders or fear of persecution. Jewish displaced persons (DPs) (known as the Sh'erit he-Pletah—the Surviving Remnant) did not want to return to the countries that had handed them over to the Nazi killing machine. DPs from many countries now under Soviet control did not want to return to face Communist rule and probable persecution. More than one million people were in this category— stateless and homeless.

Hundreds of DP camps were set up throughout West Germany, Italy, and Austria, and in the United Kingdom. From 1945 to 1952, more than 250,000 Jewish DPs lived in these camps. By October 1945, administration of the camps was taken over by the United Nations Relief and Rehabilitation Administration (UNRRA). Life in the DP camps was not easy. Food, shelter, and other supplies were often inadequate. As people were repatriated or found new homes, the DP camps were consolidated and many closed.

In the DP camps, refugees set about creating cultural and educational institutions. Many chose to marry and start new families, still mourning the families they had recently lost. Some of the camps became almost town-like, permanent homes. Refugees traveled from camp to camp, searching for surviving relatives or friends. The camps became more ethnically and religiously similar, some were nearly all Jewish.

Within the camps, a central theme that was discussed was obviously where the DPs could be resettled. Many Jews wanted to immigrate to Palestine, but quotas (like everywhere else) were strict. Belgium put in place a program to accept refugees, followed by the U.K., Canada, and Australia.

Once the State of Israel was established in May 1948, more than half a million DPs and other European refugees made their way there. Following the admission of 250,000 DPs, the United States passed the Displaced Person Act in June 1948 to accept nearly 400,000 refugees or more from Eastern Europe (100,000 of them Jewish).

By 1952, the remaining approximately 250,000 refugees had found homes and the last of the DP camps closed.

14

ARON KLEINBERG ENTERS OUR LIVES

His name was Aron Kleinberg. Aron was born on April 27, 1907, in Boryslaw, Galicia, a part of Poland where his family had lived for centuries.

Like all Jews, his family suffered greatly during World War I. The war was fought literally in their back yard. As a young boy, he saw through the kitchen window Russian and Austrian soldiers killing one another. Aron came from a large extended family. His father's name was Yehuda, and he was much older than Aron's mother, whose name was Basha.

Of his five brothers and two sisters, Aron knew what happened to only two of his brothers. One brother immigrated to America, but Aron lost track of him. The other brother, Max, went to Belgium where he survived the war with his wife and two children. Aron had the equivalent of a fourth-grade education, which was mostly self-taught, but he could speak and read Polish, German, and Yiddish sufficiently to get by.

As a young man he was also involved in the Esperanto movement—an attempt by intellectuals to create one common international language. Before the outbreak of war, Aron was married and had two lovely young daughters, both under age ten. His ambition was to own his own bakery or a restaurant, so he signed up to be an apprentice in an established Boryslaw bakery.

Aron told Mother and me of many incredible hardships he and his fellow countrymen were forced to endure after the Russians made them "join" their army. They became prisoners and labor for the Russian war machine. The Russians force-marched the men for months, traveling mostly on foot and only brief segments by truck, to Siberia, a place called Nizhny Tagil, where Aron was part of the forced labor pool that helped build tanks.

Aron worked and slept in the factory where they assembled machinery for making tanks. He had a small eight-by-four-foot space that was three feet deep. These spaces were used to assemble engine blocks from underneath. This hole in the ground was where Aron slept and ate during most of the war years.

Life was hard and had little value. He lived under constant fear of being robbed of his food ration, shoes, or anything of perceived value. Aron had several close encounters with fellow workers. One time a man whom he called a Russian anti-Semite attempted to steal a pair of Aron's gloves in the cold of winter. Luckily, Aron had a wrench in his hand, so he hit the thief over the head with his wrench and almost killed him. Another time two men were going to attack him and take his shoes, but he managed to run away and hide under a tank until the thieves left.

The men worked six to seven days a week with only a starvation diet. There was little to cheer about, except when the Red Army was beginning to free Poland. Aron did, however, meet a young Russian woman who became enamored with him and wanted to marry him. To Aron that was out of the question. He told her, "I have a wife and two children waiting for me when the war ends. I can't marry you, nor do I want to live in Russia after the war."

Once the war ended, Polish deportees working in factories in Nizhny Tagil were permitted to return home. They were being repatriated not to Galicia where they came from, but rather to the Poland with new borders. Galicia was now going to be part of the Ukraine.

Aron came back to Breslau, Poland, about the same time Mother did. He was told there were no Jews left in Boryslaw, and if his wife and two children were alive, they would most likely end up in Breslau. Aron came to the synagogue and the billboard to look for any information that would tell him what happened to his family. By then it was clear to him that no one of his family survived except his brother in Belgium.

Meanwhile the woman with whom he had a relationship in Russia came to Breslau and wanted to marry him. Her timing wasn't good. Aron had already met Mother and he was in love with her. Besides, the Russian woman wasn't Jewish, and that mattered to him. More importantly, he knew it would matter to his brother. The returning Jews from Russia were in shock and then disbelief when they saw and heard what happened to their relatives. Once the reality set in, it became clear to most that it was time to move on.

Meanwhile, the Rabbi came back with a favorable ruling in Mother's *get* from Chaskiel. When the Rabbi called all parties concerned with the *get* in his office, the group also included Aron. The Rabbi explained the Jewish law to all at the table and then asked Chaskiel to sign the paper.

Chaskiel said, "No!"

The Rabbi asked, "Under these circumstances, why don't you want to give Fajga a *get*?"

Chaskiel stood up and said, "She can have the *get*, but Mendel stays with me!" And he ran out.

Mother asked the Rabbi, "What happens if he refuses to sign since he knows that I can't leave my only son with him?"

The Rabbi said, "He did agree to the *get* but just refuses to sign a paper. Come back in a couple days and pick up your signed certificate."

"But what if he still refuses to sign?" she wanted to know.

The Rabbi smiled and said, "A couple of nights in our Polish jail, and he will change his mind."

Meanwhile, Chaskiel instructed Zlata not to hand me over when Mother and Aron came to get me.

I certainly didn't want to live with Chaskiel and his new wife and her little girls. I knew where my loyalty lay, and it was clearly, without any hesitation, with my mother. She had always been there for me.

Although I never said this to my mother, I really never believed Chaskiel deliberately left us all on that train to die. Maybe I just didn't want to believe Chaskiel was capable of such cruelty. Mother was justified in her feelings. She was convinced he was chasing a skirt and got grabbed by the Russians and conscripted into the army.

On the other hand, irregular train stops and the constant search for food farther from the train station are likely arguments that he may just have missed the train. From Mother's perspective, the fact that he had gotten married right after he left the train and now had two children told her that Chaskiel had written her and her babies off as dead.

In the end it doesn't matter. The fact is that we simply don't know for sure what really happened after he left the train. He never told us.

Chaskiel being Chaskiel, he wanted to control events to his own benefit. If he had persisted in denying my mother the *get* and giving me up, I probably would have killed him. He didn't know me and what I was capable of.

15

"LET'S GO SEE THE REST OF THE WORLD"

Both Mother and Aron came to pick me up, but Chaskiel was not at home. Zlata was polite, and she actually offered them something to drink. As she helped me pack, she said to Mother, "I am sure Mendel will have a much better life with you than he will here."

As I was leaving, Miriam started to cry. She grabbed my leg and didn't want me to leave. Zlata looked concerned when we left. She knew that there would be a price to pay when Chaskiel came home and saw that she had let me go. When we walked out the door that day, it was the last time I had any contact with the Dawidowicz family—that is, until recently.

The first time I met Aron Kleinberg was that day in Chaskiel's home. Aron was a good-looking, gentle man with a big smile. When he spoke to me, it was as if he was speaking to an adult, not just a nine-year-old child. I liked him from the start.

He took my hand and said to me, "Let's go see the rest of the world." That was in June or July 1946.

Along the way he stopped for a moment, looked me in the eyes, and asked, "I know having me with your mother might not be right with you. I don't expect much. Mendel, is there any reason why we can't be good friends?"

"I would very much like to be friends with you!" I replied.

At that time and place I needed a friend more than I needed a parent. Mother was pleased because it was apparent to her that we liked each other. Ever since that first meeting we got along splendidly. Our main focus was on getting out of Poland. But first we went to the *shul* to pick up mothers *get* papers. The *get* lay on the Rabbi's table.

He picked it up and pointed to the big X beside the signature line, "That is your husband's signature, and according to Jewish law you are now a free woman."

We walked from the *shul* to Mother's apartment where she lived with Haia. That evening the four of us talked until late into the night. We spoke of the present, the past, and the uncertain future, but mostly about Aron. He had left early to go home and pack. Haia kept telling Mother how lucky she was to find such a nice man.

She repeated several times, "I tell you, Fajga, Aron will be a good husband to you and a good father to Mendel."

Mother shook her head and said, "It's time something good happened to me."

Aron came to the apartment early in the morning. His suitcase was already in the *droshky* (carriage) parked on the street next to the building. Mother and I were also packed. I looked in my suitcase for the knife Chaskiel purchased for me, but it was gone. Chaskiel probably took it so I would come back to look for it. But it was too late, and it no longer mattered.

Mother's most valuable possessions were her *fufaika*, two bags of tobacco, and two bags of raisins. The carriage was hitched to two old horses, and all our belongings hardly took up any space. We could just as easily have walked to the station, but I think Aron was being romantic.

We drove to a Jewish Refugee Center. There we merged with other Jews who were also leaving Poland. The plan was to go to Belgium where Aron's brother lived. The best way to get there was to go to a DP camp in Germany and then go to Belgium from there. Poland was not allowing anyone out except through special arrangements. The *Brichah* (see below) had gathered enough people to fill a passenger train, and they had their own people manage the paperwork when we crossed the borders.

The Brichah Movement

Brichah is the Hebrew word for flight, or escape. The Brichah Movement refers to the organized efforts of Jewish Eastern European refugees and DPs to immigrate to Palestine prior to the establishment of the State of Israel in May 1948. At this time, Palestine was under British Mandate and such immigration was illegal.

In many cases, the Brichah first had to smuggle Polish and other refugees into the DP camps—and then plan for their clandestine travel to Palestine. Many boat-loads of the Brichah's would-be immigrants were turned back by the British authorities. In the three years of its efforts, the Brichah successfully transported approximately 250,000 European Jews to Palestine.

To Belgium

Aron's brother, Max, lived in Antwerp, Belgium. He had owned and operated the Unger restaurant in Antwerp since before the war. Max survived the war with his wife, Golda, and two young children.

How Max and Golda's Daughter Survived

In the summer of 1942 the Germans began to round up Jews in Belgium. At that time, Aron Kleinberg's brother, Max, lived in Antwerp, Belgium, where he owned and operated the Unger restaurant. Max and his wife, Golda, left for Brussels to hide. They had a sixteen-year-old son named Shimon (Simon), and he survived by being placed in a Christian children's home. While in hiding, on November 23, 1942, Yardena (Tonette), their second child, a daughter, was born. The situation was extremely dangerous for Jews in Brussels, and for a family with a baby it meant certain death for all.

Josephine Vernimen lived in Edegem and worked as a waitress in the Kleinberg family restaurant in Antwerp. Josephine, a single, young, compassionate Christian woman, offered to keep the baby hidden with her. At the time, Josephine was engaged to Frans Peeters, whom she married at the start of 1943.

To avoid any suspicion in the neighborhood, Josephine took baby Yardena to live at Josephine's mother's house at Aartsellar, near Antwerp.

Josephine's mother knew the true identity of the child, but no one else knew Josephine's secret. Josephine didn't even tell Frans after she married him that Yardena was not her own child.

Golda and Max Kleinberg with son, Simon, in Belgium before the war. Tonette (Yardena) Kleinberg with Josephine and Frans Peeters who hid and raised her during the war.

Several times Josephine risked her own life by taking the baby to visit Max and Golda who were hiding somewhere near Brussels. Yardena stayed with Josephine and Frans Peeters until the end of the war. When Yardena's parents came to claim her, Josephine's husband, Frans Peeters, refused to give her back, not believing that Yardena was not his child. The custody was settled amicably when Josephine's mother confirmed the circumstances under which they had accepted a pledge of silence.

> *Yardena was returned to her parents at about age four. She continued to visit the Peeters family on holidays and remained in regular contact with them until she immigrated to Israel in 1951. Josephine passed away before being recognized for her good deed, and Frans lived several years longer.*
>
> *Through Yardena's effort, however, Josephine and Frans Peeters are now enshrined in* Yad Vashem *(The Holocaust Museum) in Israel. They hid, nourished, and nurtured a Jewish baby during the years of war and therefore managed to save her from deportation or death. The Institute of* Yad Vashem *gave the Award of Righteous among the Nations to Frans Peeters and posthumously to Josephine Peeters.*

Max was ill, so he offered his brother, Aron, a partnership in the restaurant if he would come to live in Antwerp and help him run the business. It was a successful restaurant and generated enough income to support two families. Most importantly, this opportunity meant a normal and comfortable life for all.

In an insane and unpredictable world, Belgium seemed to be the place for us to regain our own sanity and hope for a better future. All we had to do was get there. Mother and Aron's plan was simple. Pick me up, then all of us would to travel to Germany, and there we would obtain new identity status as DPs—displaced persons. In Germany, Mother and

Aron would get married, and from there we would find our way to Antwerp, Belgium, and the good life.

In Aron Kleinberg, my mother had found a man she could trust. Theirs wasn't a love-love relationship at first. Theirs was a love of need. They needed each other to get what they wanted. A lot of marriages after the war were marriages of necessity or convenience. These were people who had lost their first family and when they found someone else they could have companionship with and start a family with, it was very hard to resist marrying. It made sense. Besides, these couples also shared a common experience of having lost a great deal, so they were more apt to cling to whatever new relationship they formed.

Aron made no secret of his motivation to marry. In fact he made it a condition of marriage that my mother must bear him children or he would leave her. He desperately wanted the family he had lost in the war. That was most important to him. While it didn't start off as a love affair, I later saw that my mother and Aron really were deeply in love and completely devoted to each other.

Later that evening we finally boarded the train, and when the train crossed the Polish border, I had a malaria attack. It is a horrible illness. First came the high fever, then the cold shivers, followed by delusions. Aron handled the crisis with concern and tenderness as though I were his own son. He wrapped me in a blanket and held me in his lap. After a while he made room for me to lie down under their bench. He even bribed some passengers with cigarettes so they would hold their luggage in their lap and leave the space under the bench for me.

Cigarettes and coffee were the main currency of that time. Aron had several cartons of American cigarettes he brought to smoke or to use for trade. He actually stopped smoking his own cigarettes but would pick up butts from the floor and roll them into cigarettes that he smoked. Aron began using his American cigarettes to trade for anything people had that would ease my pain.

In Prague we had to change trains, and although I was nine, Aron carried me like a baby wrapped in a blanket from place to place. In Hof, Germany, we changed trains again. It was strange, but the German passengers were very polite and very sympathetic to my condition. Several passengers voluntarily gave up their seats to make room for me to lie down, and one woman gave Aron a beautiful hand-woven blanket to cover me.

A man who claimed to be a doctor gave Aron some pills for me to take and told Aron to take me to a Munich hospital as soon as possible. Aron took out a pack of cigarettes to give him and the doctor said, "No. You will need these cigarettes to purchase quinine medication when your son is in the hospital."

It was a completely different Germany than what we expected. Where the hell were these Germans during the war? When we arrived in *München* (Munich), we saw that the railway station was completely destroyed and the rubble cleared, but what was once a beautiful train station was now a burned-out shell. Signs of war damage were everywhere, but we could see reconstruction work going on all over.

We were taken to a DP camp in Munich, which is located in Bavaria, of the American zone of occupation in West Germany. We were housed in what were formerly German army barracks, temporarily converted to house DP residents.

Some of the buildings were bombed-out, and others were patched up to accommodate us.

After registration Aron immediately started to press the camp authorities to get me admitted into a Munich hospital near the camp. The camp infirmary didn't have much to offer and very little medication. I spent two weeks in the hospital. Aron and Mother came to see me often. Aron used his cigarettes liberally to get me the life-saving quinine medication needed to cure me of this horrible affliction. When I came out of the hospital, I was cured and fit.

DP Camps

On October 31, 1946, we were moved again to a small DP camp located in the province of Württemberg. The name of the DP camp was Wasseralfingen. It was then located outside the larger ancient city of Aalen, also in West Germany. The inhabitants of that DP camp were all Jewish, and the DP camp had its own Jewish administration. It had a bakery, a *mikveh* (ritual bathhouse), a *kheyder* (religious school), and a public school. Most of the housing was appropriated by the American administration from the local population.

We lived on the first floor of a small duplex home. The German owners would come in spring to plant their flowers and garden. They were polite, and there was no friction between us. The camp had two gates, with a Jewish guard posted only at the front entrance gate.

Before we officially moved into the apartment assigned to us, the camp Rabbi interviewed Aron and Mother. After checking their stories, the Rabbi married them in February 1947. That month we became a family, and Aron became my father in all aspects, except perhaps legally. I loved him and called him Father.

My sister Basha (Bessie) was born on May 14, 1947, in Aalen, the nearest city to Wasseralfingen with a hospital. While other men in the DP camp were engaged in black market activities, Father, who had trained as a baker before the war, set up an ice cream stand.

Father had purchased an old hand-operated ice-cream machine. It consisted of a wooden bucket, and in the middle was a polished metal container where he poured his liquid brew. Ice mixed with salt was packed around the metal container. A metal handle sticking out of the bucket was connected to the gear. That container with the liquid in it was rotated in the ice-packed bucket until the liquid hardened and became ice cream.

In the evening he would prepare his liquid concoction, and early in the morning I would leave with my wagon to Aalen and purchase a block of ice and bring it home. It was a good two-hour round trip.

Making and selling ice cream all day long was hard work and involved the effort of the entire family. Father just wanted to get enough money together so he could hire one of those smugglers whose profession was to smuggle people and goods across the borders. He wanted to go to Belgium to see his brother, Max.

Aron Kleinberg (left) makes and sells ice cream in the DP camp.

Mother also tried to help bring in some money by working in the matzah factory during the Passover season. With our DP identification cards, we could travel legally only in the American zone of West Germany.

My years in the DP camps were very pleasant. We always had enough to eat. They provided us with a good supply of clothes. There were sports and other activities for the children and adults. I played soccer. I was very good at it, too. That was the first inclination I had that I was athletically gifted. Sports would play a big role in my life for the next few years.

We didn't always have a regulation soccer ball for our matches, so sometimes we improvised with a basketball. Boy, did it hurt to kick that big ball.

We were provided bats, gloves, and baseballs, but we could never figure out how to play the game. We had never seen baseball played before.

Class photo taken in the Wasseralfingen DP Camp, West Germany, February 1948. The author is in the first row, third from right.

During the winter of 1947–1948, Father hired a smuggler to take him illegally across the German border to Holland, and then to Antwerp, Belgium. Father was very happy to meet his only surviving brother and the rest of Max's family; however, Mother was concerned. She was fearful that something might happen and Aron wouldn't return. Or maybe he might just decide to stay there and not return. She ran around saying, "I should have never let him go."

Father stayed with Max for over a month. Max was ill and wanted Father to stay. Father said he must go back to get his family and promised to return together with us. In spring of 1948, Father hired his smuggler again. We packed the bare minimum necessities for the journey and left the apartment with everything in it for a friend to guard. Father told his friend that once he successfully arrived at his destination, the friend could report to the camp commander and keep what was in the apartment.

The smuggler's name was Maciej because he claimed his name means a gift of God and, he always added with a big grin, to women. Maciej was a slick operator who spoke seven European languages fluently. We took a train to a small village near the Holland border, and from there we made our way to the barbed wire fence that marked the border between Germany and Holland.

The border was not heavily guarded, but the police on both sides were on the lookout for smugglers. We waited at the fence until midnight when usually a change of guard took place. Maciej instructed Father, "Remember that bridge on the other side from last time? We will stay there until the break of day, and then we will make our way to that same small house we stayed last time. From there I have transportation arranged for us all the way to Max's restaurant."

Maciej was a jokester. He said, "I hope Max keeps his word and prepares for me that famous dinner I ordered!"

My father had a suitcase tied up with a rope. My mother had Bessie tethered to her. We stayed in the shadows beside the bridge before crossing an open field, single file, the moon lighting the way.

When we reached the house, the border police were waiting for us. They arrested us and threw us all together in a jail cell. Maciej drilled Mother and Father what to say and how to say it. It was important to have the same story, he told us. However, the story Maciej concocted was to save himself and put all the blame on Father. We communicated with Maciej in Polish, and we were to say that we didn't speak or understand any other language except Polish. This meant that Maciej did all the translations, and Father couldn't even contradict the lies he was telling.

Father, Bessie, Mother, and I spent three weeks cooped up in a one-room Holland jail cell. I kept Bessie occupied with games I made up with Father's hat. Maciej was let go the next day. Before leaving he said to Father, "Stick to our story. The next time we try, it will be on me, and it won't cost you anything."

By the time Father realized what just happened, Maciej was gone. After the investigation was done, we were sent back to Wasseralfingen and Father to an Augsburg jail, where he spent three months. Back in Wasseralfingen we learned that Max had died May 19, 1948. Father was devastated. He felt he should have stayed with his brother and found a way to bring the rest of the family over. Father kept on communicating with his sister-in-law, Golda, but he never attempted to make another journey to Belgium.

From that time onward our final destination plans were focused on Israel. After a two-thousand-year wait, on May 14, 1948, Israel became an independent Jewish state. The excitement and jubilation of that day in all the Jewish DP camps was hard to describe, and for many of us the mere mention of the State of Israel still evokes that heartfelt feeling. We, like thousands of other DPs, signed up to go to Israel as soon as the country could absorb us.

Unfortunately, Israel's Arab neighbors attacked, and little Israel was busy fighting for its survival. The birth of Israel brought great joy, but the war brought great anxiety, so Mother put us on a list to go to America as a second choice. In our camp, life went on as normally as the times permitted. On March 18, 1949, my younger sister Golda (Goldie) was born. It was a season of birth and hope.

Landsberg

During WWII, Landsberg was a concentration camp until discovery by the Allies on April 27, 1945. Then it became a displaced persons (DP) camp on May 9, 1945. Landsberg contained twenty-one sub-camps holding 5,251 prisoners. Ironically this is the town where Hitler was imprisoned and wrote Mein Kampf.

By September 1945, Landsberg became a Jewish DP camp with kosher meat, a Yiddish newspaper, and organized schools. It was here that nine kibbutzim *were established on farms that formerly were held by the Nazis. A* kibbutz *is a collective farm where all aspects of life are communal—money, work, property, governing. Many of the post-war Landsberg residents went on to help establish the State of Israel. David Ben-Gurion, the founder of the State of Israel, visited the camp on the day of their first democratic election. "Hatikva" was sung in Landsberg and later became the Israeli national anthem.*

16

LADY LIBERTY BECKONS

On July 27, 1949, we were transferred to the Landsberg DP camp located in Bavaria. The camp had been founded in 1945, two days after Germany had officially surrendered. The American military government had selected the former German army base, which was named by Hitler, as the location of the DP camp. It provided comfortable accommodations in the barracks for the displaced people.

The author's sisters Golda (left) and Basha in the Landsberg DP Camp, August 1950.

By the time we arrived in Landsberg, the camp's residents were all strictly Jewish. The camp was a hotbed of political activity. Yiddish slogans were on walls of every political group. "Eretz Yisrael—the State of Israel—is small, but it will grow large through your work. Speak little but do a lot!"

I was now thirteen and signed up for the metalworking apprenticeship. The first thing I learned to make was a metal hammerhead. By the fall of 1950 the inmates in Landsberg had shrunk to fewer than two thousand residents. News in the German newspapers appeared stating that the American authorities planned to dissolve the camp no later than April 24, 1951.

Soccer teams in the Landsberg and Foehrenwald displaced persons camps. This photo is from the United States Holocaust Memorial Museum, courtesy of Jack Sutin.

A view of the Landsberg DP camp. This photo is from the United States Holocaust Memorial Museum, courtesy of Herbert Friedman.

On October 25, 1950, we were transferred to Lechfeld DP camp, one of the last DP camps to remain in West Germany. Then, on February 10, 1951, we were moved again to Augsburg to await destination selection and processing.

Finally, on April 16, 1951, we were instructed to pack our bags, take one soft bag per person and one large wooden crate per family, and be ready to be transported by truck to the port of Bremerhaven. We were among the last of the camp inmates to leave. We arrived in the port of Bremerhaven on April 26, 1951.

Displaced persons departing Germany for the United States wait with their luggage in the former Von Tirpitz navy yard. This photo is from the United States Holocaust Memorial Museum, courtesy of Selig Goldberg.

A Jewish social service official poses beneath a train carrying DPs to the port of Bremerhaven, where they will board a ship for the United States. This photo is from the United States Holocaust Memorial Museum, courtesy of Selig Goldberg.

Our expectation was to be on a passage to Israel, our first choice; however, the DP camps were being eliminated, and there were mainly three countries that would take in displaced Jews: Israel, Australia, and the United States. It was by sheer chance that we ended up on the manifest of the *USS General R.M. Blatchford*. This U.S. transport ship was taking us and some 1,400 Jewish and non-Jewish DPs to New York City, with one scheduled stopover in London.

The ship's manifest lists the destination for the Kleinberg family as Boston, U.S.A. The names on the manifest are Father, Aron, age 43; Mother, Fajga, age 37 (actually 33); son, Mendel Dawidowicz, age 14; daughters, Basha, age 3, and second daughter, Golda, age 2.

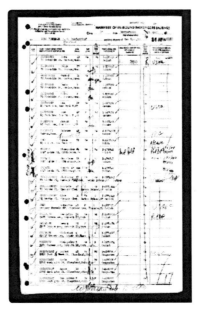

Manifest from the USS General R.M. Blatchford, *a U.S. transport ship, showing the Kleinberg family onboard headed to New York City.*

The author, then Mendel Dawidowicz, passport photo, 1951, age fourteen.

All I knew of America came from the Western movies I saw starring singing cowboys such as Hopalong Cassidy and Tom Mix. When I pictured America, those images of the Old West with cowboys and Indians popped into my head. The first black people I ever saw were American soldiers in Germany, and I thought they were Indians from America.

Our Atlantic crossing began on May 1, 1951, aboard the converted troop transport. It seemed huge, yet our tiny cabin was big enough to accommodate our family of five. It was right next to the gas tank and was always filled with a terrible smell from the gas and oil.

Our cabin didn't have beds or cots but hammocks suspended from the ceiling. They swung in place with the movement of the ship on the water.

I was seasick almost the entire voyage from the movement of the ship and the smell of the fuel. The first thing I wanted to do when I got up in the morning was head up to the deck.

I made a friend on the ship. He was a Christian Pole. When we met he said, "You're a Jew," and I said, "So what? By the way, I just want you to know in advance that if you make any comments about me being a Jew, I'll punch you."

He replied, "I don't care that you're a Jew." That sealed our friendship. We used to go up to the bow together. It was right next to the anchor. We would find a spot there that was hidden from the weather, which was cold, wet, and windy on the way across the Atlantic.

Quite often we stayed on the deck overnight. It could be quite pleasant when the weather was mild. The fresh air was a big relief compared to the stuffy environment down below.

My mother was always worried I would get lost. When my father would hear her fret about it, he'd say, "How's he going to get lost on a boat?" But the truth is the ship was so large with its various decks and nooks and crannies that you had to be very careful not to lose your way.

We stayed out of people's way, not because we wanted to but because we were too sick to be scampering about. Our nausea finally started improving as we got closer to the United States. My friend got over the sickness much quicker than I did and for a time he was dragging me around, saying, "Let's go see what's over here."

To help pass the time, we played checkers. It was my favorite game. But our main entertainment was exploring the ship. We were everywhere on it. We sort of had the run of it or at least we thought we did. The crew didn't seem to mind and left us to roam freely. Many crew members were helpful in answering our questions and directing us how to get back where we started. The other kids didn't bother us as long as we stayed out of their way and minded our own business.

The food was good. We had three meals a day. But when suffering from seasickness, who could eat?

We had no idea what America was like. All I could imagine was that it was like Argentina from the storybook Pioter, Edmund, and I had become enchanted by. In my head I saw a giant garden with orchards everywhere.

We were so ignorant about America that before we made the voyage my father wanted to buy things he thought would not be available there. He bought two Schaffhausen watches, a Leica camera, and a selection of down pillows, tablecloths, and silverware including a menorah, declaring, "That will be good currency to trade," not knowing of course how rich in material goods the United States was.

He did have a hundred dollars saved up from all those years schlepping ice cream in the camps. That was a sizable nest egg to start with considering he and my mother had lost everything to the war.

In the travels that my family and I were forced to make we were variously considered outcasts, displaced persons, prisoners, allies, refugees, and guests. The authorities, however, did not always bother to inform us what our official status was, which meant we had to guess based on the way we were treated and what was happening in the war. Because the situation was fluid and allegiances and fortunes changed so much, we could never be absolutely sure at any given point if we were regarded as friends or enemies, as wanted or unwanted visitors.

At one time or another we were branded as just about everything under the sun. We were a people without a country, adrift without a home to call our own. At different junctures we were claimed by Poland, Germany, the Soviet Union, and the Allied Forces. If not for the hatred Poles held for Jews, we would have reclaimed our Polish citizenship after the war. When it became clear Poland did not want us back, we set our sights on the newly formed Jewish State of Israel. But when going there was closed to us, we ended up voyaging to the United States and becoming American citizens.

The way our resettlement journey played out during and after the war, moving from place to place within Poland, the Soviet Union, and eventually Germany, we were like vagabonds who went with the wind. It was an epic journey in many ways. The sheer geography we covered was staggering—thousands of miles. Most of our wandering occurred in the former Soviet Union, whose vast expanse of land encompasses eleven time zones, climates, and cultures, many of which we experienced for ourselves.

We were constantly reacting to events. We never had any plans or any ideas as to what the next step was going to be. Every time we stopped someplace, we did not know what was going to happen. We did not know where we were going next until we got there. It was like being a puppet on a string. Someone else controlled everything. Being able to adapt to circumstances beyond our direction and making the best of ever-shifting conditions was crucial. It meant survival.

Now we were on the last leg of our journey to our final destination. I could hardly wait.

Displaced persons of various nationalities seeking to immigrate to the United States line the decks of a transport ship as it leaves the port of Bremerhaven. This photo is from the National Archives and Records Administration, College Park.

Welcome to America

Stewards on the ship passed out leaflets written in English, German, and Polish explaining what awaited us in America. One steward interpreted the words in German for us. He told us that in America we would have an equal opportunity to become American citizens and have the right to vote. He said the Statue of Liberty represented our right to practice our religion without interference from anyone, including the government.

My friend and I stayed up all night on deck to ensure we didn't miss what we were told was a special sight. We heard people talking about Lady Liberty. We learned that it was a big iron lady with a torch in one hand and a bible in the other.

After two stormy weeks at sea, on May 14, 1951, the sky cleared up. A stunning sunrise followed the ship as we made our way past the incredibly beautiful Statue of Liberty. When we sailed into New York harbor, we could see her in the distance. What a beautiful sight. I still get goose bumps when I think about it. She was standing there and seemed to be smiling at us. We thought it was a little statue, but as the ship got closer, we realized it was a mammoth thing. I remember thinking, well, maybe America's big too.

I remember also having the strangest feeling inside when I told myself from now on I'm not going to be afraid anymore. I just had this strong feeling that this was going to be a place where I don't have to fear anybody or anything. That day I became an American Patriot and have been so ever since.

Shortly thereafter, we landed on Ellis Island for processing.

In New York City we found out that our Boston sponsor had died, and a new sponsor was found for us somewhere in the Midwest. We had no idea why we needed a sponsor or where we were going, but it didn't matter as long it was in America. Within six weeks after landing in New York City, we were under way by train to Milwaukee, Wisconsin.

Arriving in Milwaukee was the first good day of the rest of our lives, and a good life followed us ever since.

OUR AMERICAN STORY

We were well taken care of by Jewish Family Services who rented us a house on the east side of Milwaukee, not far from the local Jewish Community Center. It was an old house. The floors were uneven from the foundation settling. But the wood-frame Victorian-style house had five rooms. We had the whole place to ourselves.

To us it was a palace filled with what we regarded as luxuries, such as a full bathroom with a shower. It had all kinds of amenities, including beautiful old furniture. Some chairs had velvet covering. For the first time in my life I had a bedroom all to myself. Also for the first time I had two pairs of socks and two pairs of underwear. I had a t-shirt, three dress shirts, a warm jacket, and new shoes. I was so pleased with those shoes that I used to walk around and look down at my feet to admire them.

The Jewish Family Services official who greeted us in Milwaukee seemed genuinely happy to see us. He embraced each one of us. He was a real estate man in Milwaukee by the name of Meister. After we got settled in our home he would visit from time to time. He liked to talk to my father. He said to him once, "You know I'm a Communist just like you." My father jumped back, a bit startled. He didn't know what to say or do. He didn't want to wind up getting sent back to Eastern Europe, which by then was under Soviet control, by seeming to be a Communist sympathizer.

The Cold War was on and the nation was hyper-sensitive to anything smacking of disloyalty. Meister filled the uncomfortable silence by saying he had been a Communist since his youth. My father finally spoke up to inquire, "But you've got your own house and business, how can you be a Communist?"

"Well, in America," Meister explained, "you can be a Communist like me. The only place to be a Communist is here. You sure don't want to be one in Russia." That was a friendly neighborhood political lesson delivered on our front porch.

The neighborhood we lived in was not Jewish at all but actually Italian. The high school I attended was predominantly black and Italian. Counting myself, there were only two Jews there. I was a good athlete so nobody hassled me. My sports were football, wrestling, track, tennis, and ping pong.

When I came to America at age fourteen I couldn't read or write any language although I spoke several. Because of all the interruptions in my schooling in Europe, I was far behind my grade level. So I was sent to a Jewish summer camp where I learned to understand English.

My father, Aron, caught on to English right away. He had no trouble. My mother, Fajga, never learned to read or write English, but of course she didn't read or write any other languages well either. The most she could do was sign her name. My father was not as encouraging as he could have been about her continuing her education. That was probably one of my few contentions with him.

I tried to help her the best I could. I told her, "You can do it." Sometimes I would sit down and work with her, and she would work diligently, but my father would discourage her. He feared she would make a fool of herself trying to become educated and possibly become a target for anti-Semitism. His fears were unfounded.

Soon after our arrival, Jewish Family Services found my father a job at a Pontiac dealership. Later, they found him a better job at the Allis-Chalmers factory, a manufacturer of heavy equipment. My mother wanted to go to work but my father wouldn't let her. When my siblings and I were older, she did begin working in a frozen potato pancake manufacturing plant.

The spring after our arrival in America was the first time just the five of us celebrated Passover together in an intimate family setting. During our time in Germany there were communal Passover celebrations at the DP camps. They were held in a big hall with all kinds of people around.

But for our first Passover in Milwaukee, Jewish Family Services brought over some Mogen David wine, gefilte fish, Maxwell House Haggadah books, and a glass seder plate. My mother bought a new tablecloth for the holiday, and she laid it out with the glass seder plate. We were all sitting there with tears in our eyes. This was our first seder as a new family.

I remember everything about that seder. We had some macaroons; we had matzah. It was a custom in our family for my parents to break off a piece of the matzah at the beginning of the seder and hide it away for one of us children to find. The hidden piece is called the afikoman. The seder cannot go on without it. Once the child finds it, then the parents buy it back with some money or a prize. As the youngest child, my sister Goldie, had that privilege for our first Passover seder in America.

Sitting around the table as a family we proclaimed and prayed that night, "This is our new family and home. From now on we're going to grow and prosper." When my father was retiring for the evening, I overheard him say something that had a big impact on me: "We're all that's left. We've got to put what happened in Europe behind us and go forward." Those words and sentiments guided me.

That first year I wanted a bicycle so badly because my friends all had their own bikes, but I understood that we didn't have the money for it. My father suggested we could find a used one and that's what we did. He helped me restore it and make it almost like new. I got a job delivering the *Milwaukee Journal Sentinel*. Before long I saved up enough money to buy a brand new bike of my own.

After my brother Eugene was born in Milwaukee, the first American-born family member, our family became six. I loved having brothers and sisters. I hoped my parents would have a dozen children.

(Left) Bessie, Mother (Fajga) holding Eugene and Goldie in Milwaukee, 1954. (Right) Bessie, Goldie, and Eugene, 1954.

If there is anything that I have learned about life it is that family is everything. Relationships are everything.

Fitting In

There were some things I had to contend with as a newcomer to America. At the beginning some kids mocked me about my accent. There were a few push-and-pull confrontations but nothing serious. They knew I was an immigrant and most didn't care. Besides, I lived in an Italian neighborhood and most of the adults in those Italian families were immigrants themselves.

I absorbed Americanism like a lost soul in the desert absorbs water. I probably lost my accent better than my refugee friends.

One of the ways I assimilated quickly was by being unafraid to do things with the guys, whether playing sports or hanging out or cruising the streets. I just mixed in with them and became a part of the action. I was also busy because I had to work my paper route to help support the family. Later I got on as a clerk at one pharmacy and after I left there I worked for another pharmacy. I was a quick study.

When I enrolled my freshman year at age fourteen, however, I could hardly read and write. I despaired that I would not be able to last. I was fortunate that I was invited, with two other refugee boys, to be tutored by a Polish woman on the south side of Milwaukee. She was a retired principal. She was tasked with getting us ready for school.

We came to her in May and school started in September. The other boys, Sam and Aaron, could both read Yiddish. Aaron had been sent to the Yeshiva school in Chicago. Sam was three years older than I and could read and write Polish. I couldn't do anything, except I knew the alphabet.

The tutor gave me special instruction. She was very kind and honest. She said, "I can only take you so far because there's so much you don't know." She gave me several volumes of an old Durant series on the history of the world (the title was *The Story of Civilization*). She challenged me to read it during the summer. She also gave me a dictionary and told me that whatever I didn't understand to look up its definition.

That whole summer, wherever I went, I read, if not the Durant series then something else—newspapers, magazines, signs, anything. She told me I would catch on fast, and I did.

Even with all that work behind me she told me flat out, "Your chances for graduating are not good." She marked down in my records that I graduated from grade school, which I hadn't, to avoid school officials placing me a few grades back.

My athletic prowess is what really made it possible for me to advance in school. I would never have finished high school otherwise.

Even though the game was completely foreign to me, I signed up to play football that freshman year. I could really run and so naturally I was made a running back. But I didn't know what a running back did. The coach gave me some simple advice, "When you get the ball, run like hell." That's exactly what I did. I also signed up for wrestling, tennis, and ping pong, where I excelled.

Because I showed such promise on the gridiron, the coach assigned a couple girls to tutor me. I think the first two semesters they passed me out of pure kindness. Plus, I didn't create any problems for anybody. But the second year I pulled my own weight and I was right on track academically. By my third and fourth years, before graduation, I was getting Bs and B-pluses.

I went to a public high school, Lincoln High. A male math teacher there encouraged me to stay with math and that proved very fruitful to me in my future studies and career. He was also helpful advising me because I was confused about everything.

I told him one day, "I have a lot of catching up to do." I was referring to my lack of education because of all those years in Uzbekistan and then in DP camps. I told him some of my story including how my father, Chaskiel, had abandoned us.

He asked, "Do you have any feelings for your father's name?"

I said, "Absolutely not."

So he suggested I "change everything," including my name.

I enlisted the help of an attorney friend of the family and filed court papers to change Mendel Dawidowicz, officially and forever, to Milton Mendel Kleinberg. Milton just seemed close enough to Mendel, and it didn't hurt that Milton Berle was a beloved Jewish comedian appearing on the new boxes in everyone's homes called television.

Lincoln High School, Milwaukee, ninth grade class picture, 1951. The author is on the far right in the second row.

Meeting Marsha

After high school, I entered the U.S. Army in 1955 and came out in 1958 after serving in Korea.

The author served in the U.S. Army from 1955 to 1958 in Korea.

When I was on leave back in Milwaukee, I met Marsha Paykel at a local Jewish Community Center. Saturday nights the place was jammed with young adults. She was seventeen. I was in my early twenties.

The way Marsha remembers it, she was expecting me to show up because a mutual friend had told her I was going to be in town on leave. I was not in uniform, but she tells me what attracted her attention was my dark curly hair, which sadly is all gone today. She said I had kind of a Sal Mineo look, referring to the popular movie actor at the time. We made small talk that evening but did not see each other again until my release from the military.

By then, Marsha was in college when we resumed our acquaintance at a Hillel dance.

I didn't come from a family of means, and when I was on my own, I was always working lots of jobs just to get by. I drove second-hand cars or what Marsha referred to as clunkers. They were not always dependable. When she and I were dating, it seemed as if every single time we went out we had to get the car battery jumped.

I had little spending money, and Marsha had even less. My clothes were hardly fashionable or new. I would wear a jacket from one suit and pants from another. Nothing matched. But we were happy. And we married on August 14, 1960, in Milwaukee.

During our early years, our daughter, Cindy, was born. Our son, Hershel, named after my brother who died in Samarkand, was born three years later. While the children were still in school, Marsha went back to school for bachelor's and master's degrees in speech pathology.

When I was in high school the former U.S. Olympic decathlon gold medalist Bob Mathias, who became a preacher and motivational speaker, came and spoke to us. He said some words I have been repeating ever since: "There isn't anything I have done that any one of you can't do. The only difference between me and you is the 10,000 hours I've put into it."

That inspired me. I wanted to be good at something. I wanted to be successful. That same motivational message comes out of my mouth all the time: You are what you think you are, so think positive. To succeed you must first shed the fear of failure, and then get in the habit of doing those things that failures refuse to do. The world belongs to the doers so be a doer! It's become like a mantra for me.

I wanted to be able to make a good living. That was very important to me. I felt it was my obligation but more importantly I wanted people to be proud of me, and I was willing to do anything within reason to make a success of myself. I tried a lot of things, not always successfully, but I tried them. I was a factory worker at American Motors. That was the job I got right out of the Army. I owned an ice cream store. I painted and remodeled homes and offices. I painted church steeples. I would go paint in places nobody else wanted to touch. Everybody was afraid of wasps in the eaves of those churches and houses, but I climbed up those ladders and got the job done. I worked in a lumberyard. I also sold copy machines, and restaurant supplies.

One of my most important accomplishments was becoming a naturalized citizen of the United States of America, which I did on May 1, 1959.

My life took a new direction when I was at John's Bargain Stores in Milwaukee for the big sidewalk sale. I was there putting my wares out and selling things to people. A guy from Southwest Insurance saw me and said, "Hey you, I want to talk to you." In me he saw a salesman. He saw someone who liked to talk to people and could earn their trust. I was very persuasive. He made me an offer to join the company in 1964, as an insurance salesman.

Later, when I saw that his company didn't have much going for it, I left and became a debit agent with Prudential. From there I perfected my sales skills and built R K Insurance, Inc., a life and health general insurance agency of fifteen agents. We marketed products for ITT Life Insurance in eastern Wisconsin. The insurance agency was successful, and it grew to thirty-five agents, which made it possible for me to expand from a two-state operation to a multi-state marketing company, representing major national insurance companies.

Marsha was a speech pathologist and worked for the Milwaukee school system from 1973 to 1978. When the children were older, I made Marsha an offer she couldn't refuse. She quit teaching and became the office manager in our business.

Opposing Hate

My identity as a Jew was impressed upon me during the war when merely being a Jew was reason enough for state-sanctioned genocide. The experience my family and I had being exiled to a strange and distant land just because we were Jewish made me think about what it means to be a Jew. When you are born a Jew, you know you're a Jew. Sometimes that means being defensive.

Anti-Semitism is a heavy burden. Living with anti-Semitism continuously is like having lice. It sticks to you all the time; it itches all the time, but if you can find a way to free yourself, you find a great freedom.

Living in the U.S., I was far removed from the most virulent anti-Semitism but not completely free of it. When the American neo-Nazi party became active in Milwaukee in the 1970s, I helped form the Concerned Jewish Citizens (CJC), an organization to counteract the activities of this hate group. The white supremacists wore Nazi uniforms, brandished the swastika, and spoke and marched at various settings throughout Milwaukee. Their presence was an offense and a challenge to any decent-minded person but especially to a Jew. Their hurtful symbols and language opened old wounds.

One of those Nazi characters lived across the street from a synagogue whose Orthodox Rabbi survived the concentration camps. A pack of that cowardly Nazi gang harassed Rabbi Feldman one day. They pulled his beard and spit in his face. The incident was an outrage.

Some of us were so worked up about it and so convinced that we needed to take action before something more serious happened that we got together to organize CJC. We met in my house and decided we were going to respond to the Nazis rather than stand silent or lie down. Many of us had learned hard, tragic lessons and sacrificed far too much during the Holocaust to allow these haters to get a foothold in our city, in our neighborhood. There was no way I was going to be complacent in letting history repeat itself. Not on my street. Not if I could do anything to stop it.

We did our homework. We learned that the Nazis met in certain restaurants and would try to recruit the people who ate or worked there. We found out they had a regular meeting on the south side. One night a group of us activists went in the parking lot of the meeting hall when the Nazis were inside and wrote down all of the vehicles' license plate numbers. I actually went into the meeting hall while they were there, and they promptly recognized me and roughly escorted me out.

But notice had been served that we were watching them. We told them in no uncertain terms, "You're not going to get away with this." Every place they went, we were right behind them. A few times we went nose to nose. Once, a couple of their members used baseball bats to smash the window of a car I was in with two others of our group. I pulled out a .45-caliber revolver I kept on me and pointed it at them, and that changed the situation. They dropped the bats and got out of there. We received threatening phone calls at our home and my attitude was, "C'mon over." I would not be intimidated. They would not make me a prisoner in my own home.

We raised quite a bit of stink in the community. Some elements of the local Jewish community were not too happy with us. They viewed us as troublemakers who were only making matters worse.

They said, "The Nazis are a bunch of nuts, leave them alone and they'll go away."

We from CJC said, "No, we're not going to leave them alone. I saw with my own eyes how that passive, naïve approach led to atrocities in Europe."

Our organization was active for about two years. During that time we even started a newspaper we printed up and mailed out from our basement.

The Nazis left Milwaukee and resurfaced in Skokie, Illinois, where they planned to march in that heavily Jewish community. Residents there were divided about what to do. My activist friends and I went there to confront the Nazis as needed and to rally counter demonstrations. We went to churches, synagogues, and other groups and organized resistance as best we could.

Lots of words flew. There were lawsuits and threats of violence. It became a heavily publicized showdown. Later, a made-for-TV movie titled *Skokie* came out. In the end our tactics worked, and the Nazis left Skokie with their tails behind them the same way they'd left Milwaukee.

Shining a light on evil and calling it what it is—that's the only way to address it. Evil can only exist when good people let it.

My involvement with Concerned Jewish Citizens was not the first time I put myself out there in a public way. Marsha and I co-hosted a Sunday morning radio program in Milwaukee called the Call of the Shofar. We presented and commented on Jewish news from around the world.

We saw a need for a Jewish program on a day of the week when there were many Christian shows but no Jewish shows. We bought the airtime for the show ourselves. Marsha was always in my corner, but sometimes my outspokenness was even a bit much for her, not to mention our listeners, who didn't always agree with my strong opinions. But after what happened to me and my family and to millions of Jews in the war, I simply would not keep silent about things I perceived to be wrong.

Our Family Grows Once Again

My career path in insurance began at that sidewalk sale when I was recruited by an insurance company. Over the years, I worked for different companies selling life and health insurance. I traveled throughout Wisconsin in my territories and talked to farmers and people of all endeavors. That's how insurance was sold.

Some of the companies I represented weren't always successful, but I was. I built my reputation by operating my agency based on moral and ethical principles. We always tried to do what was right for our agents, the insureds, and the insurance company. I didn't adopt these principles to prove some moral point, but rather because it made good economic sense over the long run.

Opportunities in life came in unexpected ways. In 1984 Colonial Penn lost its contract with AARP to provide members supplemental health insurance policies. So in 1985 Colonial Penn offered an exclusive contract to an Omaha marketing company called Senior Market Sales, Inc., "SMS," to market Medicare Supplement policies nationally through an agent distribution system. It turns out that the SMS owners didn't have any knowledge on how to market Medicare Supplements. They were skilled in marketing life insurance, which required a much different strategy.

By then I had already earned a national reputation of integrity and sound performance in the Medicare Supplement marketplace. I was invited by SMS owners to come to Omaha for a consulting meeting to discuss how to proceed in developing a national marketing strategy to sell Medicare Supplements through an agent distribution network. The discussions were cordial, but I quickly realized that the owners had no understanding of the senior marketplace. And I wasn't sure that they even wanted to know what it would take to launch this project.

When I flew back to Milwaukee after that meeting, I told Marsha, "I'm going to own that company in Omaha." Shortly after that I purchased 50 percent of SMS.

Then for five years, I began to commute, on a weekly basis, from Omaha to Milwaukee. By 1990 Marsha and I officially moved to Omaha. Shortly afterward I purchased the rest of SMS, and Marsha became the office manager.

My father, Aron, lived into his mid-eighties. He worked hard for Allis-Chalmers all those years in Milwaukee. I guess that "training" program making tanks for the Russian

Army was helpful. My mother lived a full and happy life surrounded by five generations of family and friends, She passed away in 2012 just two weeks shy of age ninety-eight. She had lived her years in Milwaukee where my sisters and brother were there to help. She never was able to read or write and consequently never passed the test to become an American citizen, which she regretted.

Life Is Good

So, you see, in America life was good for the Kleinberg family. We preferred not to dwell on the past, just to look forward to what this great country has to offer to anyone willing to work hard and play by the rules.

I like to say our family insurance business became an overnight success, after fifty years of perseverance and hard work by my wife and me. At my seventieth birthday party, Marsha and I truly realized how blessed we were to have such wonderful family, friends, and business affiliations at this stage of our lives. And for that we are immeasurably grateful to the Almighty and to this magnificent country of ours.

When people hear me speak in glowing terms about America, I am often asked, "What is so great about America?" My answer is that I have seen the rest of the world. And the more I have seen and experienced the rest of the world and its history, the more I have come to venerate America and the great nation it has become. Churchill's comment on democracy is also apt for America. We may not be the most perfect nation, except when compared to all the other nations of the world.

When our grandson Yossi was married in 2010 in Israel, the family from America joined relatives living in Israel. We attended the dedication of a stone statue carved by Shosh Ha Levi in honor of our relatives who were victims of the Holocaust.

The ceremony was held outside of the Testimony House at Beit Haedut before an audience consisting of family and friends of the Dawidowicz family. Moving and emotional speeches were given in Hebrew by some attendees. I was also asked to give a speech. It was a good thing I couldn't understand Hebrew. Otherwise, tears would have been pouring from my eyes and I wouldn't have been able to deliver my speech, given by me in English and my grandson in Hebrew.

I began, "Shalom. My name is Milton Mendel Kleinberg; however, I was born Mendel Dawidowicz on January 28, 1937, in Pabianice, Poland."

EPILOGUE

When I applied for Social Security benefits in 2002, the clerk asked to see my birth certificate. I told him I had none because it was lost during the war. He then gave me the address of the Polish Embassy in Washington, D.C., and told me to send a request for my birth certificate, which I did. I never expected to get a response.

To my amazement and surprise, I received my birth certificate written in Polish. The birth certificate stated I was actually born on January 28, not January 1, as my mother had told me. In fact, I was surprised to learn that I was actually born in 1937. Why was I surprised? Because my mother had given me an earlier year of birth in the DP camps so I would qualify for the daily glass of milk and a paczki (donut) given to the older kids. Her gifts to me continued to keep on giving.

Further, for the first time I learned the correct Polish spelling of my parents' names and my mother's maiden name. This meant I had enough basic information to start a search for family roots in Poland.

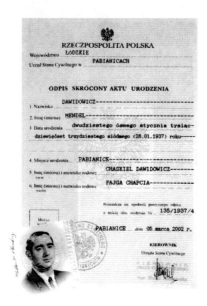

The author's official birth certificate.

My Search for Family Roots

My search for family roots began on October 8, 2008, when I saw an ad in Hadassah magazine placed there by Michael Goldstein, who listed himself as a professional Jewish genealogy searcher. I immediately called and followed up our conversation with an email containing the basic background information about the Kleinberg and Dawidowicz families. We communicated back and forth by email and phone. Just two weeks later, Michael emailed me the following information:

I met yesterday with two of the children of Yechezkel (Chaskiel) Dawidowicz. There is no doubt that they are your half-sisters. They knew much less about the early history than you know and told me that their parents never talked, and their father was a dreyer. Dreyer is a Yiddish word, which can translate as elusive but it is much more and can come from the word turn. To confuse the issue, the word dreyer really means someone who spins a yarn. That was the second time I heard that word.

Your father worked as a shoemaker here. One sister has vague recollections of you from after the war. There were six children. Five are alive, four daughters and a son. There was another son. He took sick after they came [to Israel in 1951] at about age 1. He went to the hospital and was never seen again. They were told that he died but no death certificate or burial location was ever found. They believe that he did not die but was one of the children who were alleged to have been "stolen" from their parents in the 1950s and adopted by others.

It appears that at that time quite a few children were taken from their immigrant parents and given for adoption to parents who lost their children during the Holocaust.

Chaskiel must have picked up the profession of shoemaker in Russia. Before the war he was a fierman, hauling cargo by horse and wagon. After the war, Mother commented after hearing that Chaskiel was working as a shoemaker, "At least this time he picked up something useful for the family."

Michael also commented during our phone conversation that Miriam and Shoshana Dawidowicz told him Chaskiel had a passion for pigeons, and that resonated with me. My mother and I hated those smelly pigeons, and they were a source of contention between my parents. All these little bits of information about Chaskiel added up to the genuine personality I recalled. No other individual could have been so similar for it to be a coincidence.

Finally I accepted the fact that Michael had found Chaskiel's children, and I now have four more sisters and one more brother living in Israel. I was both exhilarated and confused at the same time. Stories like this are what Academy Award movies are made of.

Once we established there was definitely a family connection, Michael informed me that my sisters and brother in Israel would like to have a face-to-face meeting, and would I be interested?

It so happened that Marsha, my son Hershel, and I, were going to Israel to attend our grandson Zev's wedding. The wedding was held on January 4, 2009, in Jerusalem.

Michael arranged a meeting for all of us in his Jerusalem apartment. Needless to say this was a very emotional meeting. I spoke Yiddish with Miriam and Shoshana, and Michael translated what we were saying in Yiddish to the others in English and Hebrew.

The last time I had seen Miriam and Shoshana was 1946 in Breslau, Poland, when they were babies living with Chaskiel and their mother, Zlata. As I recall, Shoshana was in a buggy, and Miriam was holding on to me as I pushed the buggy. There was a lot of conversation and reflection. The growing family had remained in Poland until they sailed to Israel in 1951, just as the Kleinberg family sailed for America.

I wanted to know what happened to Chaskiel. They said he died in Israel in a bad way. He was a laborer and he got hit with a pipe or something. Apparently he was never the same after that. They wanted to know more about their father. They said he never told their mother he had any other children. They didn't know about me. It was a big shock to them. They didn't know there were others besides me. They didn't know that he didn't try to come back for us. It turned out they also had issues with him, but he was their father. They wanted to know more.

I realized it was time to tell the stories.

My life stories unfolded in remarkable ways. For example, Marsha didn't know Aron Kleinberg was not my biological father until our wedding day. We were at the synagogue for the ceremony. The *ketuba* or wedding contract is signed by the man and his father, and after I signed it, I was going to have my father sign it when one of the groomsmen who had also come over from Europe spoke up and said, "Well, that's not your real father."

I told him to be quiet for now and that I would explain later, rather than have him spoil the moment. That was the first Marsha ever heard of it. I later explained what happened but spared her the details and therefore the complete truth. For example, I told her my birth father may have ended up in the Russian Army and was killed in the war. In fact my brother, Eugene, and sisters, Bess and Goldie, didn't know that I was their stepbrother until my mother told them when Goldie was undergoing a divorce. Mother just wanted to ease Goldie's pain by confessing that she too understands her sadness.

My rationale for keeping the full story from Marsha and my family was that when I came to America I made a pledge to myself that I was going to put the war behind me, that I was not going to dwell on the past, and that I was going to start a new life in America. My whole attitude was that the past was the past and I didn't care to look back.

It's a terrible thing if you feel like a victim. I had a friend who was a survivor and he lived the Holocaust every day because he felt he was a victim. My attitude about people is simple—all people are essentially the same, the only difference among them is how they see the world. If you think you are a victim, then that's what you are. Victimhood is paralyzing. If you think you can't do something, then you won't try.

But the idea here in America is that you don't have to live or die how you were born. You can move, you can advance, you can change your attitude, and, by doing so, you can change your circumstances.

Survivors who come here are in two groups. There are those who never stop talking about the past, and there are those who go to their grave never talking about it and whose children never learn anything about it. We knew many survivors in Milwaukee whose children never learned anything from their parents about their Holocaust experiences.

It was only after our kids were grown that I began to open up more about my past. Sometimes a little something would come out. When I talked to our grandkids, I would reveal a little something more.

When I began working on this book, Marsha became my gentle reader and most trusted critic. As I shared passages with her to review, she finally learned the true extent and scope of my childhood survival experiences. Among other things she learned how I really got those scars and why I was always fascinated with knives. It all stems from the knife in Samarkand, the bandit, and the kidnapper.

The impetus for doing the book began when my children and grandchildren wanted to know how my parents and I survived the war. That subject came up often across the *Shabbat* dinner table. In my mind, I had the story written but couldn't put it on paper until I knew some of the details of names and cities that were revealed when I received my Polish birth certificate.

When my grandchildren were in high school, they went to Poland to visit Holocaust sites. They called me asking, "Hey, Grandpa, we're going to be near the place you were born, can you tell us something about it?" Putting my story on paper started in earnest with their questions.

So between discovering my half-sisters, the questions from my grandchildren, and my willingness to finally tell the complete story, especially to Marsha, who was always encouraging me to write my story, I decided to write this book. Thank you for reading it.

TEACHER'S GUIDE

THE TESTIMONY OF MILTON KLEINBERG (MENDEL DAWIDOWICZ)

The opportunity to bear witness to survivor testimony whether by reading diaries or memoirs or hearing it in person is not to be taken lightly. Those who survived the Holocaust are burdened with the urgency to tell their stories so that the millions who perished are not forgotten. The receiver of the testimony bears the responsibility of remembering and sharing the message so the world does not forget and allow the same atrocities to happen again.

The testimonies are as varied as the survivors themselves. Each should be considered a precious piece of history. While the suffering of survivors should never be compared, it should be understood that each experience was traumatic and life altering. The impact did not end when the survivor was allowed to leave his or her place of incarceration. Each time the survivor shares his or her story, it takes an emotional toll on that person.

Readers may be familiar with stories involving concentration camps or people in hiding. Milton Kleinberg's memoir takes the reader on a 7,000-mile train ride to labor camps in the Soviet Union and life in an orphanage. He steps out of the safe environment he knew in Poland and enters a world where he is forced to be resourceful and engage in behavior one would never expect from a young child.

Milt Kleinberg originally wrote his story as a memoir for his grandchildren. He wanted them to know his story and the events that shaped his early years—as well as those that occurred for many Polish and Jewish Polish citizens during World War II.

A memoir is distinctly different from a diary. A diarist records what is happening at the time with no idea of how the story will end. Diaries became companions for some, not intended for others to read. Others saw their diary as a stream to the future as documentation of history.

A memoir is written after the fact. The memoirist knows the whole story, reflects on memories, and relives poignant, frightening, and traumatic times of the past. The memoirist has had time to reflect on what has happened and decides what experiences he or she will share with the reader and how to share them. Pieces of history or information can be included that might not have been known to the author at the time the experiences were happening. In looking back, the memoirist can bring some understanding to the story of his or her life. The memoir is the story of a person's life—memories, feelings, and insights.

BOOK CLUB STUDY QUESTIONS

Chapters 1-3

1. One of the tactics of the Nazis was to dehumanize the Jewish people. List examples in these chapters that illustrate that tactic. Continue to find examples as you read the book.

2. Anticipate how the harsh life of Chaskiel and Fajga is preparation for what lies ahead.

3. Despite Chaskiel and Fajga's lack of formal education, they trusted their own assessment of the situation and acted accordingly. Summarize how their perspectives differ from that of Chaskiel's father and the Rabbis.

Chapters 4-5

1. The people on the train were not being deported only because they were Jewish. What were other reasons for deportation?

2. How were Chaskiel's fighting instructions to Mendel an example of dehumanization? How has war changed how one must cope?

3. "Our bundles were packed with the most practical things we could carry." Clearly the deportees did not pack as we would if we were traveling. What kinds of things did they pack? What was the reasoning behind the items they did pack?

4. In chapter 5 the storyline takes the reader from checkers and other games to dead bodies and eating rats. As incongruous as checkers and other games sound, explain why they were important and even necessary to the boys.

Chapter 6

1. Dignity is a theme in chapter 6. List ways that the passengers and, more specifically, Fajga, tried to maintain their dignity.

2. Anti-Semitism existed on the train. "Yet after the Leningrad stopover, we families in the boxcar got to know each other. The sharp difference between Jew and Christian disappeared …" How could these events be an endorsement for getting to know others, to break down barriers, and to reinforce the idea that we are more alike than different?

3. A former teacher tries to hold school for the children on the train. Explain how this exemplifies hope and belief in the future.

Chapters 7-8

1. Arrival in Samarkand meant adjusting to new people and new ways. What acts of kindness did Fajga experience with the death of Velvel? As a Polish prisoner?

2. Explain why Fajga would give up a job that meant more food rations, better living conditions, and a measure of dignity for harder work in the tobacco factory.

3. Mendel says a "code developed on the playground." What was that code? What kinds of playground codes have you experienced?

4. "Stealing from work and bribery were a way of life in Samarkand." Why was this a necessary way of life? How does this relate to the dehumanizing talked about in earlier chapters?

Chapter 9

1. Mendel is arrested for leaving the children's home and stealing apples. He tells his mother, "You don't have to worry about me! I can take care of myself." Her response is to slap him so hard he is knocked off his feet. Explain her quick and harsh response.

2. A school in a forced labor camp may seem unusual. What was the intended purpose of the school?

3. Food rations for children as they are described in this chapter may seem inadequate. The reality was that "life was at the most primitive stage." Explain what this means.

Chapter 10

1. Hunger nearly becomes a character in the memoir in chapter 10. What statement about hunger sticks with you? Why?

2. Mendel and his friends arm themselves. What is your reaction to the killing of the Uzbek? How were children capable of doing this act? How has their world changed?

3. Malaria, typhoid, and DDT are terms that are not associated with developed countries. Research one of these terms and write a paragraph about it.

4. At the end of the chapter Edmund learns that his mother is alive and it changes his behavior. Think of others you have learned about thus far in the memoir who have lost a family member. How does death or survival impact the individuals?

Chapter 11

1. Edmund is kidnapped, and Pioter and Mendel jump into action. When Edmund is safe, the boys say they were "shaking with excitement" and "jumped up and down screaming 'We are heroes! We are heroes!'" What were the unrealized dangers for the boys? How do you explain the euphoria the boys seem to be experiencing?

2. "The war was always on our mind." "Hunger set the daily agenda." Despite the war and their constant hunger, the boys were able to carry on discussions about topics such as movies, politics, and their lives after the war. How do you explain their ability to talk about these "normal" things in such adverse conditions?

Chapter 12

1. The war had ended but Mendel was still in Samarkand, Uzbekistan. His mother is faced with yet another choice. Keep Mendel with her or let him return to Poland with the rest of the children. What concerns must she be wrestling with as she makes a choice?

2. "We had been just small children when the Nazis rousted us from our homes. Now we were older boys, about nine years old … We were different." List two experiences the boys have had since leaving Poland and how you think they have made the boys "different."

3. Upon arrival in Moscow the children were treated "as if we were children of dignitaries." What was the Soviet motivation for such treatment?

4. What fears follow Mendel as he rides the train back to Poland?

Chapter 13

1. Being reunited with family members should bring joy. What are some of the complications for Mendel and his friends as they learn about family members?

2. Today we have the Internet and other means of communication to locate missing people. Describe the process in Breslau, Poland, and the frustration it must have caused when trying to locate family members and friends.

Chapter 14

1. Aron Kleinberg's war experience is still another perspective. Describe how he spent his war years.

2. Describe how Mendel believes his father became separated from the family. How does this differ from his mother's conclusion?

3. Mendel's fierce loyalty to his mother is evident at the end of this chapter. His statement that Chaskiel did not know what he (Mendel) was capable of is a very strong statement. At this point he is no longer in a situation of starvation and a daily struggle for survival. Do you believe Mendel is capable of such drastic actions? Why or why not?

Chapter 15

1. In the aftermath of the war, the parameters of marriage had changed. Describe the change and explain why this happened.

2. "My years in the DP (Displaced Persons) camps were very pleasant." Many people believe that once the war was over, life returned to normal for everyone. What do you think the impact of several years in a DP camp might have on people?

3. Based on the brief mention of Israel in this chapter, explain your thoughts on the importance of the State of Israel to the Jewish people.

Chapter 16

1. After living in a series of DP camps, Mendel's family is on its way to America. What ideas do Mendel and Aron have about America?

2. Upon arriving in America, Mendel has the "strangest feeling inside" that he would not have to be afraid anymore. When have you been afraid? What would it be like to live with fear for years?

3. What does the Statue of Liberty mean to you?

American Story

1. Mendel came to America without a formal education or being able to read or write any language. This was not uncommon for Holocaust survivors. What would be some of the everyday challenges of not knowing the language of the country in which you live?

1. Go to one of the following websites and learn about Passover traditions Mendel (now Milton) describes.
http://www.jewishvirtuallibrary.org/jsource/Judaism/holidaya.html

   http://www.interfaithfamily.com/holidays/other_holidays/Jewish_Holidays_Cheat_Sheet.shtml

2. Milton's experiences during the Holocaust made him an advocate for standing up against what is wrong. List examples of Milton being an up-stander after his arrival in America.

Epilogue

1. After so much loss during the Holocaust, Milton is connected with four additional sisters and one additional brother born to his biological father. How would you react to learning you had additional siblings? Would you choose to meet them? Why or why not?

2. Many survivors chose not to share their stories for many different reasons. Why did Milton choose not to tell his wife the whole story until he wrote this book? What might be reasons other survivors chose not to tell their stories?

WRAP UP ACTIVITIES

I. *Lebensraum*—the German word for living space. Using a map of World War II Europe, color code by year the expansion of the Third Reich in Europe as the Germans created "living space" for Germany. Link to map: *http://www.fsmitha.com/h2/map10eu.htm*

II. Anti-Semitism. Fajga understood that anti-Semitism was deeper than name-calling and discrimination. Read the following United States Holocaust Memorial Museum links on anti-Semitism. Write an essay showing your understanding that anti-Semitism was not something invented by the Third Reich.

http://www.ushmm.org/confront-antisemitism/antisemitism-the-longest-hatred

http://www.ushmm.org/wlc/en/article.php?ModuleId=10007166

http://www.ushmm.org/wlc/en/article.php?ModuleId=10005175

III. Fajga is an amazing and interesting person. Select three events from the memoir that reveal Fajga's character. Describe the event and explain the character trait that Fajga demonstrates.

GLOSSARY

afikoman – (Hebrew) a piece of matzah broken off at the beginning of the Seder meal and hidden for the children to find, eaten as "dessert" at the end of the seder

anti-Semitism – prejudice, hatred, or discrimination against Jews simply because they are Jewish

artisan – craftsperson, a skilled manual worker

Aryan – a race of people described as Into-European; the Nazis believed Aryans represented a "pure" race

bazaar – the market, an open-air trading place

bayonet – a knife or sword attached to a rifle muzzle

bema – in Judaism, the platform on which religious services are conducted

Black Plague – a devastating illness that brings Black Death, germ carried by fleas on rats

Blitzkrieg – (German) lightning war, massive invasion with planes, tanks, and troops

blood libel – a false claim that Jews kidnapped Christian children for their blood to use in religious ceremonies commissar – a Soviet official

dreyer –(Yiddish) a manipulator, a liar or cheat

droshky (ies)– (Polish) an open four-wheeled, horse-drawn carriage

Esperanto – the attempt to create one language known as Esperanto that could be spoken by people throughout the world

fierman – (Yiddish) one who hauled various types of merchandise or passengers by horse and wagon

frum – (Yiddish) pious

fufaika – (Russian) jacket or coat

fumigate – to use smoke or fumes to disinfect or kill pests such as lice

garbushkas – (unknown) end pieces of bread, heels

genocide – deliberate killing of a group of people (race or religious group, for example)

get – (Hebrew) a Jewish document of divorce

Haggadah – Jewish book containing passages that deal with the Exodus; gives the order of the Passover Seder

Hillel – Jewish college campus organization

Judenrat – Jewish leadership/council; appointed by the Germans to implement their directives in the Ghettos/occupied territories

Kaddish – mourner's prayer

kheyder – (Yiddish) religious school

kibbutz – (Hebrew) communal settlement; socioeconomic system based on joint ownership of property, shared work and consumption; primarily agricultural

kisloye-moloko – (unknown) sour milk, buttermilk

kolhoz – (Russian) collective farms

malaria – disease carried by mosquitoes infected with a parasite, which causes high fever, chills, muscle pain, and headaches; can come in waves; can be fatal

manifest – list of people and cargo on a ship

mantra – an often repeated phrase; words to live by

matzah – unleavened (flat) bread eaten by Jews during Passover

mavens – (Yiddish) experts

mikveh – (Hebrew) ritual bathhouse

NKVD – Russian police; similar to the modern KGB

paczki – (Polish, pronounced like punch-key) donut or pastry

pogrom – (Yiddish, Russian) massacre or persecution of an ethnic or religious group, particularly aimed at jews

rebbe – (Yiddish) a revered religious leader (Rabbi)

resettlement/relocation – term for deportation, often to killing centers

schlepping – (Yiddish) dragging or hauling, often slowly or awkwardly

Seder – feast commemorating the exodus of the Jews from Egypt, celebrated on the first night or the first two nights of Passover

Shabbes/Shabbat – (Hebrew) Jewish Sabbath, a day of prayer and a refrain from many types of work

shah – (unknown) quiet, "hush"

Shamah/Shema – (Hebrew) a Jewish prayer

sheygets – (Hebrew) non-Jewish or gentile young boy

shochet – (Hebrew) ritual slaughterer of animals

Shofar – a ram's horn used for Jewish religious purposes

shtetl – (Yiddish) village

shul – (Yiddish) Jewish house of worship; synagogue or temple

tallit – (Hebrew) Jewish prayer shawl

vagabond – one who travels from place to place with no specific home

Yiddish – the language of Jews in Central and Eastern Europe; a mixture of Hebrew and German

zetskiy-sadik – (Russian) kindergarten

zloty – Polish money

TIMELINE

1918-1939

Second Polish Republic, Jews recognized as a nationality; rights protected by the Treaty of Versailles although largely ignored

1933

January	Hitler appointed Chancellor of Germany
February	*Reichstag* fire
March	Dachau is established; Enabling Act passed
April	Boycott of Jewish shops

1934

German-Polish non-aggression pact meant to last ten years. Germany pulled out in April 1938

1935

Nuremberg Racial Laws

1936

Germany remilitarizes Rhineland

1937

January Author Mendel Dawidowicz (Milton Kleinberg) born in Pabiance, Poland

Polish Foreign Minister Josef Beck states Poland has room for only one half million Jews, the other three million must leave (also known as the Madagascar Plan)

1938

March Anschluss – Austria is annexed by Germany

July Evian Conference – thirty-two nations met to discuss how to handle the German-Jewish refugees; only the Dominican Republic agreed to accept more refugees; the United States and Britain did not; Intergovernmental Committee on Refugees (ICR) was established

September Germany is given the Sudetenland of Czechoslovakia by Britain, France, and Italy

November 9–10 Kristallnacht (Night of the Broken Glass), mass riots burn synagogues and vandalize Jewish-owned businesses throughout Germany

1939

May–June Voyage of the *St. Louis* – 937 passengers left Hamburg sailing to Havana, Cuba, and the United States refused entry. All sailed back to Europe. Some entered other countries; 254 did not survive the Holocaust

August Nazi-Soviet Non-Aggression Pact – each nation vowed not to attack the other

September Germany invades Poland; as a result, World War II begins

October Nisko-Lublin Plan called for the expulsion of Jews in German-occupied areas to the Lublin region of Poland, a transit camp was set up in Nisko

November Lodz (where the second largest population of Jews in Europe lived) incorporated into the Third Reich

1939–1940

Russians begin Sovietization of newly acquired territories with collective farms, redistribution of private and public Polish property

1940

January Author's family's apartment and possessions are seized, they are put on a two-day train ride to Siedlce, spend one week in the burned-out synagogue, take boat across river Bug to Brest. Arrested a few days later and sent by truck to Bialystok, now prisoners of the Soviet Union. Spend one month in a holding camp.

February	Ghetto in Pabianice is closed
	Author's family boards a Russian train for deportation to Arkhangelsk, Russia, arrive approximately one month later
	Auschwitz-Birkenau concentration camp established
May/June	Author's brother Velvel born in Arkhangelsk

1941

January	Author's fourth birthday, gets in fights at school every day
Summer	Author's family forced to leave Arkhangelsk, board boxcars for train trip to unknown destination (presumed to be Central Asia) as Russians move forced labor farther from the front where war is being fought with Germans; spend a month en route to war-ravaged Leningrad
June	Germany invades the Soviet Union
August	Author's family leaves Leningrad, begins arduous two-month train trip
September	Siege of Leningrad (lasts 900 days)
	Author's father, Chaskiel, gets off the train and does not return
October	Abandoned family spends week on train in Tashkent, Uzbekistan (in Central Asia) waiting for a clear railroad track
	Author's family arrives in Samarkand, Uzbekistan. Infant brother Velvel dies, Mother works in the cotton mill

December	Japan attacks Pearl Harbor in Hawaii and the United States enters the war

1942

January	Wannsee Conference – top-ranking Nazi and German officials gathered to discuss and implement the "Final Solution"
	Author's fifth birthday, brother Hershel is four years old
Summer	Author's Mother gets job as a model for the art studio; she is twenty-four years old
Fall	Author and his brother are enrolled in the zetsky-sadik (Russian for kindergarten) at the art center
November	Soviet counter-offensive at Stalingrad drives back the German line

1943

Spring	Mother chooses to begin working in the tobacco factory so that she will be able to steal tobacco for bartering and bribing
	Hershel dies of malaria at age five; author moves to a Polish children's home run by American Joint Distribution Committee, an orphanage for refugee Polish children, especially Jewish children, spends time with Pioter and Edmund in secret meeting place called "Argentina"

April-May	Warsaw Ghetto uprising
November	Russian forces liberate Kiev

1944

Spring	Author sees bandit kill a farmer, retrieves the knife
June	Allied Forces invade Normandy, France (D-Day)
Summer	Mother gets her *fufaika* (fur coat)
August	Polish resistance in Warsaw uprising
September	Lice epidemic in the children's home

1945

January	Battle of the Bulge; death march of 60,000 Auschwitz prisoners to Wodzislaw; Russian forces secure German East Prussia
March	Allies cross the Rhine River
April	Russians reach the outskirts of Berlin
Spring	Author and friend Pioter save Edmund from being kidnapped
May	Germany surrenders, Victory in Europe Day declared
August	U.S. drops atomic bombs on Japan; Japan surrenders, marking end of World War II

1946

Spring	Author and other children leave the Polish Children's Home on a train bound for Breslau, Poland, via Moscow

July	Author arrives in Breslau, Poland; reunited with Chaskiel
Fall	Author and family move to displaced persons camps in Munich and near Aalen, West Germany

1947

January	Author is ten years old
May	Sister Bessie is born
Winter	Father Aron travels to Belgium

1948

Spring	Author's family tries to smuggle into Belgium; they are arrested and sent back to Germany
May	Israel becomes a State

1949

January	Author is twelve years old
March	Sister Goldie is born
July	Family transferred to Landsberg DP camp

1951

May 1   Kleinberg family begins their trans-Atlantic journey from Bremerhaven, Germany, to New York, New York, U.S.A., pass by the Statue of Liberty on May 14, arrive at Ellis Island

July   Travel by train to Milwaukee, Wisconsin

[Editor's note: Dates are often approximate and subject to the author's memory.]

ACKNOWLEDGMENTS

This story was not easy to tell, and I needed a great deal of encouragement and help. I want to thank the following:

My wife, Marsha, who not only encouraged me to write this story, but also endured the many rewrites and proofing of each version. Without her help, the story would never have been completed.

My mother, Fajga Kleinberg, for allowing herself to go back to those painful memory days.

My sisters Goldie Pekarsky and Bess Duckler who were helpful in extracting the information from our mother.

My daughter, Cindy Levy, son, Hershel Kleinberg, and grandson, Zev Levy, for their valuable input.

Particularly Clara Hoover who was extremely helpful in the final editing of my story.

Michael Goldstein for his genealogical research that uncovered my siblings residing in Israel.

Chad Carstensen, who arranged the photographs and restored some of them that were burdened with old age. In addition, Chad developed the map of my incredible journey.

Laura Wehde for her assistance in production.

The staff of Concierge Marketing in Omaha—Lisa Pelto, Rachel Moore, and Ellie Pelto as well as Sandra Wendel and Leo Adam Biga—for helping me edit the memories of a young boy into a marketable form to be used in education.

To early critical readers and educators: Amy Tasich, English teacher, Elkhorn South High School; Ryan Mueller, history teacher, Wahoo High School; and Jane Erdenberger, Ethnic Studies, North High School.

Liz Feldstern and Donna Walter of the Institute for Holocaust Education for supplying the historical context and opening new audiences for my story and those of others so new generations of Americans will never forget what happened to us.

ABOUT THE INSTITUTE FOR THE HOLOCAUST EDUCATION

The Institute for Holocaust Education (IHE) is a nonprofit located in Omaha, Nebraska. The IHE assisted in the creation of the historic and educational components of this book and views Milton Kleinberg's first-person account as a vital part of teaching about World War II, the Holocaust, and the life-altering events that affected so many millions of people.

The IHE provides educational resources, workshops, survivor testimony, and integrated arts programming to students, educators, and the public, as well as support to Holocaust survivors in eastern Nebraska.

IHE community programming aims to educate current and future generations on the lessons of the Holocaust, through arts and humanities events, commemorations, and testimony by Holocaust survivors and liberators. Schools and other organizations are invited to contact the IHE directly to arrange such an event, either in person or via distance learning.

Supplementing the organization's educational outreach, the IHE offers two traveling exhibits that are available for rent to museums, synagogues, schools, and other locations, as well as two static exhibits that are available to the public year-round (at the Jewish Federation of Omaha and at the Strategic Air and Space Museum in Ashland, Nebraska).

The IHE's work with educators helps to fulfill the mission of making sure the lessons of the Holocaust are not forgotten and by helping teachers more effectively educate students on such difficult historic events—both the Holocaust itself as well as other examples of genocide.

For more information, readers are invited to contact the IHE:

Institute for Holocaust Education
333 South 132nd St.
Omaha, NE 68154
(402) 334-6576
info@ihene.org
www.ihene.org

ABOUT THE AUTHOR

Milton M. Kleinberg is Chairman and CEO of Senior Market Sales, Inc., an Omaha-based insurance marketing company that provides insurance solutions for an aging America. The company was founded in 1982. Under his leadership, the company has thrived in an ever-evolving senior market by staying on the cutting edge of technology, developing products to meet a changing marketplace, and devising innovative marketing techniques.

His company now serves over 20,000 independent agents writing hundreds of millions of dollars in life and health insurance premium each year worldwide. SMS employs people throughout the United States and Israel, and is one of Omaha's fastest growing companies.

Kleinberg has served as a special advisor to Congress on insurance reform. He also holds positions on many carrier and industry association advisory boards. He is the author of a popular, informative handbook on *Social Insurance*

Solutions For An Aging America: Exploring The Past, Present, and Future of Social Security, Medicare, and Medicaid.

Despite his accolades and success in the insurance industry, Kleinberg still maintains his agent licenses and certificates and serves an active client list. He feels he cannot properly serve the agents his company contracts with unless he himself is in the field selling the same products.

When asked about his success, Kleinberg likes to say, "After fifty years of hard work, I became an overnight success."

Today, Kleinberg still runs his company and travels extensively with his wife of over 50 years, Marsha. He enjoys writing, but he can also be found hustling handball games at the Jewish Community Center in Omaha or playing golf and has no plans to retire.

Milt and Marsha Kleinberg are generous philanthropists giving of their time and expertise to unselfishly serve their religious and local communities. They support a number of nonprofit organizations and charitable causes including the Jewish Federation of Omaha, Chabad House of Nebraska, The Salvation Army, Beth Israel Synagogue, Friedel Jewish Academy, Bellevue University, the American Israel Public Affairs Committee (AIPAC), United Way, the Omaha Public Library, and the Omaha Food Bank.

Kleinberg has begun speaking about his Holocaust experience at schools and synagogues and for the Institute for Holocaust Education. He is dedicated to carrying on the memory of the Holocaust so that future generations can better understand what happened—so that it never happens again.

INDEX

AARP 195
Abraham (dying man from synagogue)29, 133
Allied Forces 177, 228
Allis-Chalmers factory 183, 195
American Joint Distribution Committee 93, 227
American Motors 190
American neo-Nazi party 191
Anders Army 111
Anschluss 224
Anti-Semitism.5-8, 31, 60, 120, 135, 148, 183, 191, 211, 217
Argentina 99-125, 176, 227
Atlantic Ocean 21, 39, 69
Auschwitz (Auschwitz-Birkenau) *see also concentration camp* 131, 226, 228
Australia 144, 173
Austria 13, 39, 144, 147, 224
Bamaul 65
Battle of the Bulge 228
Beck, Josef (Minister of Foreign Affairs) 13, 224
Beit Haedut 197
Belarus 21, 25, 39, 130
    Brest 25, 34, 39, 225
Belgium 144, 147, 155-166, 229
    Aartsellar 156
    Antwerp 156-159, 164
    Brussels 156
    Edegem 156
Belzec *see also concentration camp* 132
Ben-Gurion, David 167
Berle, Milton 187
Black Plague 5, 219
Black Road 93-120
Bohemia 13
Bolshevik Revolution 75, 100
Bolsheviks 24
Bremerhaven Port 171, 178, 230
Brest Bridge 25
Brichah (The Brichah Movement) 155
Britain 20, 121, 224
Call of the Shofar (radio program) ...194, 221

Canada 144
Caspian Sea 21, 25, 39, 69, 127, 130
Catholic Church 5
Central Asia....46-51, 65, 74, 91, 127, 226
Chapcia, Azriel 7
Chapcia, Ber 7
Chapcia, Bine 7
Chapcia, Fajga (Mother) 1-260
Chapcia, Hava (Grandmother) . 7, 9, 252
Chapcia, Hendel 7, 16, 28
Chapcia, Miriam 7, 138, 153, 201
Chapcia, Reb Gabriel (Grandfather) .7, 8
Chapcia, Sheindel 7, 10, 28
Chapcia, Wolf 7
Chapcia, Yente 7, 10-12, 28
Chaplin, Charlie 121
Chelmo *see also concentration camp* .132
China 54, 74
Christian 60, 156, 194, 211, 219
Churchill, Winston 196
Colonial Penn 195
Communists/Communism12, 27, 61, 101, 141, 143, 182
Comrade Evan 76
Comrade Manager 78
Comrade Teacher 79
Comrade Vladimir (Superintendent of zetskiy-sadik) 84-90
Concentration Camp10, 12, 31, 116, 129, 131, 167, 192, 226
    Auschwitz (Auschwitz-Birkenau) 131, 226, 228
    Belzec 132
    Chelmo 132
    Dachau 12, 223
    Landsberg 167, 169-171, 229
    Majdanek 132
    Sobibor 132
    Treblinka 132
Concerned Jewish Citizens (CJC)191-194
Cuba 225
    Havana 225
Czar Nicholas II 100
Czechoslovakia 13, 224
    Moravia 13

Sudetenland............................ 13, 224
Dachau *see also concentration camp*...12, 223
David (superintendent of Polish project) 95, 104, 113-123
Dawidowicz, Chaskiel (Yechezkel) (Father)2, 10-12, 29, 64, 135-154, 187, 200-202, 209, 210, 214, 226, 229
Dawidowicz, Fajga (Mother) *see also Chapcia, Fajga*............................1-260
Dawidowicz, Hershel........1, 14-17, 26-59, 64-98, 130, 137, 227
Dawidowicz, Mendel *see also Kleinberg, Milton Mendel*...........................1-260
Dawidowicz, Miriam........7, 138, 153, 201
Dawidowicz, Moshe.......... 10-12, 27, 253
Dawidowicz, Shoshana Rosa138, 201, 253
Dawidowicz, Velvel 41, 50, 58, 65, 71-75, 90, 130, 137, 211, 226
Dawidowicz, Zlata138-140, 150-153, 202
D-Day.. 111, 228
Displaced Person Act...........................144
Displaced Persons (DP) camp10, 142-144, 158, 167-178, 215, 229
   Foehrenwald.....................................170
   Landsberg................. 167, 169-171, 229
   Lechfeld...171
   Wasseralfingen............... 161-166, 239
Dominican Republic............................224
Dzerzhinsky, Felix..................................45
East Prussia................................. 116, 228
Eastern Europe18 ,80, 122, 145, 155, 182, 222
Edmund . 98-135, 176, 212, 213, 227, 228
Enabling Act................................... 12, 223
English (language)64, 178, 182, 197, 202, 232
Esperanto movement................... 148, 220
Estonia ....
   18, 21, 25
Evian Conference.................................224
Finland............................18, 21, 25, 39, 69
Foehrenwald *see also DP camp*...........170
France.................... 20, 111, 121, 224, 228
   Normandy................................ 111, 228
   Reims..122
German (language) ..5, 90, 147, 178, 217, 219, 222
Germans1-5, 19-36, 45, 51-54, 61-63, 73, 90, 142, 156, 160, 217, 220, 226
Germany. 5, 11, 13, 18-20, 120, 144, 155, 158-183, 217, 223, 224-230
   Aalen 161, 229
   Augsburg 166, 171

Bavaria 160, 169
Berlin.. 25, 228
Hamburg..225
Hof..160
Münich...................................... 160, 229
Posen..12
Rhine River..228
Rhineland..224
West Germany......... 144, 160-171, 229
Württemberg......................................161
Goldstein, Michael..................... 200, 231
Hadassah (magazine)...........................200
Haia 89-95, 105, 123, 141, 154
Halevi, Shoshana........................ 197, 253
"Hatikva" (song)..................................167
Hebrew (language)............5, 14, 197, 222
Hitler, Adolf.... iii, 11-13, 18, 24, 27, 122, 167, 169, 223
Holland..164-166
Holocaust.. 5, 10, 132, 192, 197, 201-207, 216, 217, 225, 233
Hopalong Cassidy 174
Intergovernmental Committee on Refugees (ICR)................................224
Iran...111
   Tehran..111
Israel......... 5, 144, 155, 166-177, 215, 229
   Jerusalem 202
Italy.. 144, 224
ITT Life Insurance 190
Japan.................................18, 54, 227, 228
Jehovah's Witnesses............................131
Jewish Community Center181, 188, 236, 251
Jewish Family Services............... 181, 183
Jewish Refugee Center 155
Jewish 1, 5, 11, 13, 14, 30, 36, 75, 95, 103, 111, 144, 150, 155, 161, 166, 170, 193, 209, 215, 219
   Orthodox Judaism................... 14, 192
John's Bargain Stores 190
Judenrat 20, 220
Kaddish (mourner's prayer) .. 30, 73, 220
Kazakhstan................................... 65, 127
   Aktau Port 127
   Alma Ata..69
   Almaty...
65
   Ganyushkino............................ 127, 130
KGB (Committee for State Security)..32, 221
Kharkiv (factory) 45
Kleinberg, Aron (Father)147-164, 173, 182, 195, 203, 214, 215, 229, 249, 251, 254

Kleinberg, Basha (Bessie) .. 147, 162, 165, 169, 173, 184, 229, 249, 251
Kleinberg, Eugene184, 203, 249, 251, 254
Kleinberg, Fajga (Mother) 1-260
Kleinberg, Golda (Goldie). 156-157, 166, 169, 173, 184, 203, 229, 231, 249, 251, 254, 258
Kleinberg, Hershel189, 202, 231, 251, 253, 254, 257
Kleinberg, Max 147, 156-166
Kleinberg, Milton Mendel *see also Dawidowicz, Mendel* 1-260
Kleinberg, Shimon (Simon) 156, 157
Kleinberg, Yardena (Tonette) 156-158
Kleinberg, Yehuda 147
Kleinberg Levy, Cindy189, 231, 245, 251, 254, 255, 257, 258
Korea 188, 246
Koscielna Street 12, 15
Kristallnacht (Night of the Broken Glass) 224
Landsberg *see also concentration camp and DP camp* 167, 169-171, 229
Latvia 18
Lebensraum (living space, German) ... 11, 12, 217
Lechfeld *see also DP camp* 171
Lenin, Vladimir 100
Levy, Yossi 5, 197, 254, 257
Levy, Zev 5, 231, 254, 257, 258
Lincoln High School 187
Lithuania 18
Luftwaffe 47, 62
Maciej (smuggler) 165-166
Madagascar Plan 224
Majdanek *see also concentration camp*132
Marx, Karl 100
Marxist 31, 32
Mathias, Bob 189
Medicare Supplements 195
Mein Kampf 167
Meister 182
Mexico 101
Milwaukee Journal Sentinel 184
Mineo, Sal 188
Molotov, Vyacheslav (Soviet Foreign Minister) 18, 61
Nazis ... 9-12, 25-38, 80, 93, 112, 125, 131, 141, 167, 192, 209
Nazi-Soviet Non-Aggression Pact (Ribbentrop-Molotov Pact)13, 18, 20, 61, 223, 225
Nisko-Lublin Plan 225
NKVD (People's Commissariat for Internal Affairs) 32, 35, 38, 61, 71, 221
Nuremberg Racial Laws 14, 224
Operation Barbarossa 73
Palestine 112, 142, 144, 155
Passover 163, 183, 216, 220, 221
Kleinberg (Paykel), Marsha 188-196, 202-205, 231, 236, 248-258
Pearl Harbor 45, 227
Peeters, Frans 156-158
Pioter 98-135, 176, 213, 227, 228
Poland .... v, 1-39, 60-67, 78, 89, 120, 123-135, 147, 155, 177, 197, 199, 202, 205, 208, 213, 214, 224, 225, 228
Boryslaw, Galicia 147, 149
Breslau 124, 130, 133, 141, 149, 202, 214, 228
Krakow 6
Lodz 13-25, 75, 134, 142, 225
Lublin 62, 225
Pabianiceiii, 1, 4, 10, 13-19, 25-28, 39, 114, 123, 142, 197, 226
River Bug 21, 24, 28, 33, 39, 225
Siedlce 24, 39, 225
Startsive 7-10
Szestochowa 89
Terespol 24
Warsaw 2, 6, 19-25, 228
Warszawska *see also Poland, Warsaw* 15
Wodzislaw 228
Polish (language). 15, 38, 56, 72, 85, 101, 134, 165, 178, 186
Polish Army 19-21, 73, 112
Polish Corridor iv
Polish Delegatura 90
Polish Embassy 199
Pontiac 183
Pravda (newspaper) 129
Protestant Reformation 5
Prudential 190
R K Insurance, Inc. 190
Rabbi Feldman 192
Reichstag (German parliament) .. 12, 223
Roma (Gypsies) 131
Romania 18, 39, 130
Rosh Hashanah 19
Russia6, 25, 39, 45, 54, 122-130, 149, 226, 245
Arkhangelsk39-49, 67-69, 90, 129, 226
Bialystok 35-39, 90, 129, 225
Kremlin 128
Leningrad (St. Petersburg) ..39, 45-53, 64, 69, 211, 226

Moscow.25, 45-54, 122, 127-133, 213, 228
Nizhny Tagil.............. 45, 148
Novosibirsk.......... 64, 72, 130
Omsk.................64
Perm..................64
Siberia.............. 32-56, 96, 148
Sverdlovsk (Yekaterinburg)...... 64, 69
Vladivostok........................54
Volga River.........................57
Vologda.............................53
Russian (language).38, 72, 76, 83-85, 90, 101
Russian Empire.........................6
SS (Schutzstaffel) *see also Nazis*........5, 24
Senior Market Sales, Inc. (SMS) 195, 235
Shabbat/Sabbath..............8, 15, 204, 221
Shemah (Jewish prayer)........................29
Siege of Leningrad.......................226
Silk Road................ 74, 93, 127
Skokie (movie) 193
Sobibor *see also concentration camp*..132
Soviet Union 18, 32-35, 45, 62, 69, 90, 101, 111, 121, 129, 177, 208, 225, 226
Soviet-German pact 35
Sovietization................... 31, 225
Soviets (Russian Red Army)18, 21, 31, 35, 40, 54, 73, 128
Stalin Ural (factory) 45
Stalin, Joseph (Soviet Premier)32, 45, 95, 100
Stalingrad, Battle of.............................227
Statue of Liberty.................. 178, 215, 230
The Story of Civilization.........................242
Surviving Remnant (Sh'erit he-Pletah)143
Tadzhikistan...........................48
Tatars (Tartars).............. 80, 117
Testimony House at Beit Haedut.......197
The Cold War....................182
Third Reich *see also Nazis* 217, 225
The Three Musketeers 98, 121, 134
Tom Mix................ 121, 174
Trans-Caspian Railway......................127
Trans-Siberian Railway 53, 69
Treaty of Versailles....................... 11, 223
Treblinka *see also concentration camp*132
Trotsky, Leon 32, 100
Tsar Alexander III 54
Turkestan-Siberian railway (Turk-Sib)65
Ukraine 45, 149
Kiev........................ 111, 228
Unger Restaurant 156
United Kingdom....................144
London..................... 122, 173

United Nations Relief and Rehabilitation Administration (UNRRA) 144
United States of America (U.S.A.) 5, 190
Boston, Massachusetts.......... 173, 179
Ellis Island 179, 230
Hawaii........................ 45, 227
Los Angeles, California............. 54, 69
Milwaukee, Wisconsin.. 179-205, 230, 249, 251
New York City, New York.... 173, 179
Omaha, Nebraska........... 195, 233, 235
Skokie, Illinois................................193
St. Louis, Missouri.........................225
Washington D.C............................247
United States Army (U.S. Army)188-196, 246, 247
United States Holocaust Memorial Museum. 4, 24, 37, 125, 131, 170, 171, 172, 178, 217
Universitet, Bulvari 81
Urals............... 48, 51
Uri................... 86, 90, 95
USS General R.M. Blatchford..............173
USSR 38
Uzbekistan.. 48, 69, 74, 77, 125, 187, 213, 226
Samarkand.. 68-91, 114, 124, 129-142, 189, 204, 211, 213, 226
Tashkent 68, 74, 91, 127, 226
Vernimen, Josephine 156
Victory in Europe Day (VE Day)122, 228
Vishinski, Andrei 111
von Hindenberg, Paul..........................11
Von Tirpitz Navy Yard........................172
Wannsee Conference..........................227
Warsaw Ghetto Uprising 228
Wasseralfingen *see also DP Camp*161-166, 239
Western Europe................. 5, 142
World War I (WWI)iii, 6, 7, 11,18, 19, 27, 147
World War II (WWII).....i, iii, 6, 7, 9, 13, 45 54, 121, 123, 143, 167, 208, 217, 225, 228, 233
Yad Vashem 26, 128, 158
Yiddish (language)5, 9, 14, 38, 56, 90, 142, 222

GALLERY

Charcoal drawing created by Cindy Levy depicting the train station in Russia at a whistle stop on the way to Samarkand.

Milt in the US Army - Ft. Belvoir, VA (1955)

Milton served in the Army from 1955 to 1958 and served in Korea.

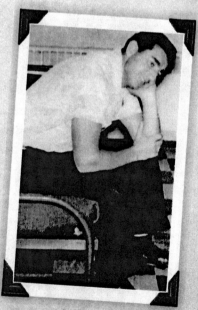

In the barracks getting ready to go into town. (1956)

Milt also served in the Wisconsin National Guard - Nike Guided Missle Site

Milt (middle) and army buddies in Washington D.C. (1956)

August 14, 1960 - Milt and Marsha's Wedding

Milt and Marsha Kleinberg Wedding
Anshe Sfard Synagogue, Milwaukee, Wisconsin - August 14, 1960
Kleinberg Family (left to right) Eugene - brother, Goldie - sister, Bessie - sister,
Milt and Marsha, Fajga and Aron - parents.

Slaves to fashion at an insurance gala (circa 1966)

Michael and Cindy Levy Wedding
Jewish Community Center, Milwaukee, Wisconsin - August 31, 1980
First Row: (left to right) Goldie Pekarsky, Bessie Duckler, Milton Kleinberg, Elliott Duckler, Melissa Pekarsky, Cindy and Michael Levy, Fajga Kleinberg, Mark Wilets, Aron Kleinberg, Rachel Paykel, John Wilets, Esther Kleinberg, Eugene Kleinberg
Second Row: Mike Pekarsky, Mike Duckler, Dan Wilets, Diana Wilets, Marsha Kleinberg, Max Paykel, Hershel Kleinberg, Al, Gordon and Bob Paykel.

Milton and Marsha Kleinberg

*The Gathering of Friends and Family for Milt's 70th Birthday Party
Chabad House, Mequon, Wisconsin, January 28th, 2007*

The Dawidowicz Family Reunion in Jerusalem
(left to right) Hershel Kleinberg, Moshe Dawidowicz, Marsha Kleinberg, Zipora Ran, Milton Kleinberg, Chaya David, Shoshana Ha Levi, Mariam Karni and Maya Ran (kneeling)

Found famliy after a 62-year separation!
(From left to right) Zipora Ran, Moshe Dawidowicz, Milton Kleinberg, Mariam Karni, Shoshana Ha Levi, Chaya David.

Kleinberg Five Generation Picture. 1st Row: (left to right) Bess Duckler, Goldie Pekarsky, Fajga Kleinberg, Milton Kleinberg, Eugene Kleinberg holding granddaughter Chava Morgenstern. 2nd Row: Shachar Levy, Mike Duckler, Avishai Levy, Cindy Levy holding grandson Noam, Maayan Levy, Marsha Kleinberg, Simi Morgenstern, Hannah Kleinberg holding niece Chia Morgenstern, Liza Eisenstock, Max Tatman, Melissa Tatman holding son Aron. 3rd Row: Zev Levy, Yossi Levy, Michael Levy, Natanel Levy, Simcha Morgenstern, Dani Eisenstock, Hershel Kleinberg.

Five generation picture at Levy home in Glendale, WI 2009.
Front Row: Fajga and Milton Kleinberg
Back Row: Liza Eisenstock - great-granddaughter holding her son,
Noam - great-great-grandson,
Cindy Levy - granddaughter

Trip to Spain (circa 2010)

Avishai's Bar Mitzvah - October 9th, 2010
Front Row: Zev and Shachar Levy,
Second Row: Natenal Levy, Marsha and Milt Kleinberg, Maayan Levy,
Third Row: Hershel Kleinberg, Yossi and Shani Levy, Cindy Levy, Avishai Levy,
Michael Levy holding Noam Eisenstock, Dani and Liza Eisenstock

Wedding of Maayan Levy to David Machness, August 14, 2012
Back row (left to right) Avishai Levy, Noam Eisenstock, Daniel Eisenstock, Liza Eisenstock, Nevo Levy, Shani Levy, Yosi Levy, Natanel Levy, Zev Levy. Front row (left to right) Gordon Paykel, Robert, Milton and Marsha Kleinberg, Cindy Levy, Maayan Levy Machness, David Machness, Michael Levy, Shachar Levy, Goldie Pekarsky.

*Fishing for uruk in the stream - Samarkand, Uzbekistan
by Maayan Levy Machness, granddaughter of Milton Kleinberg*